# ENDORSEMENTS

"Some Christians (and pastors) excel in afflicting the comforted while others comfort the afflicted. Few have the grace to do both. The prophet Isaiah was one of those who could, and reading these pages based on his great prophecies will convince you that Dr. Derek Thomas has learned to be another. Here is a spiritual treat, giving us both an exalted view of the majesty of God and a deep sense that Christ's grace is sufficient for all our needs. *Strength for the Weary* is simply a feast of good things—truly nourishing spiritual fare, skillfully prepared and lovingly presented."

—Dr. Sinclair B. Ferguson
Teaching Fellow
Ligonier Ministries

"Derek Thomas is one of the few men in the world who can blend the highest degree of biblical and theological scholarship together with the most insightful, practical, and pastoral wisdom and grace and do it in such a way that everyone can understand and benefit from it. *Strength for the Weary* is Derek Thomas at his best. If you are a Christian, you can be sure that you will experience struggle and opposition in this life. Jesus told us it would be so. That is why you need to read this book. And, as you do, you will find your heart warmed, your soul encouraged, your mind expanded, and your faith strengthened. You will find the help that you need as you strive to walk by faith and not by sight in every situation of your life."

—Dr. Guy M. Richard
Executive Director
and Assistant Professor of Systematic Theology
Reformed Theological Seminary, Atlanta

"One of the things I have long admired about Derek Thomas is the deliberate way he seeks to comfort weary Christians with clear biblical teaching. Drawing from select passages in Isaiah, Dr. Thomas combines the insights of a theologian, the skill of a preacher, and the concern of a pastor in a devotional book written for the purpose of encouraging downtrodden pilgrims. I needed this book. I suspect you do as well. Reading these straightforward but carefully crafted meditations on God's Word may not provide immediate relief from your pain. But this book will direct you to the God of all comfort. For that reason, Derek Thomas' *Strength for the Weary* is a much-needed resource for finding lasting rest in a world of constant sorrow."

—Dr. John W. Tweeddale
Academic Dean and Professor of Theology
Reformation Bible College, Sanford, Fla.

# STRENGTH

## FOR THE

# WEARY

DEREK W.H. THOMAS

ℝ *Reformation Trust*  A DIVISION OF LIGONIER MINISTRIES, ORLANDO, FL

*Strength for the Weary*
© 2018 by Derek W.H. Thomas

Published by Reformation Trust Publishing
A division of Ligonier Ministries
421 Ligonier Court, Sanford, FL 32771
Ligonier.org                    ReformationTrust.com

Printed in Crawfordsville, Indiana
LSC Communications
March 2018
First edition

978-1-56769-864-0 (Hardcover)
978-1-56769-920-3 (ePub)
978-1-56769-921-0 (Kindle)

Cover design: Faceout Studio
Interior design and typeset: Nord Compo

Unless otherwise noted, Scripture quotations are from the ESV® Bible (The Holy Bible, English Standard Version®), copyright © 2001 by Crossway, a publishing ministry of Good News Publishers. Used by permission. All rights reserved.

Scripture quotations marked NASB are taken from the New American Standard Bible® (NASB), Copyright © 1960, 1962, 1963, 1968, 1971, 1972, 1973, 1975, 1977, 1995 by The Lockman Foundation. Used by permission. www.Lockman.org

Scripture quotations marked (KJV) are from the King James Version. Public domain.

**Library of Congress Cataloging-in-Publication Data**

Names: Thomas, Derek, 1953—author.
Title: Strength for the weary / Derek W.H. Thomas.
Description: Orlando, FL : Reformation Trust Publishing, 2018. | Includes bibliographical references and index.
Identifiers: LCCN 2017036642 (print) | LCCN 2017045199 (ebook) | ISBN 9781567699203 (ePub) | ISBN 9781567699210 (Kindle) | ISBN 9781567698640
Subjects: LCSH: Consolation. | Fatigue. | Rest—Religious aspects—Christianity. | Consolation—Biblical teaching. | Bible. Isaiah—Criticism, interpretation, etc.
Classification: LCC BV4905.3 (ebook) | LCC BV4905.3 .T45 2018 (print) | DDC 248.8/6—dc23
LC record available at https://lccn.loc.gov/2017036642

In memory of J. Alec Motyer
1924–2016
Scholar, preacher, pastor

# CONTENTS

Weariness in the Christian life is something we all experience at some stage or another. Sometimes, it is impossible to give a reason for the exhaustion we feel. We are just *tired*. Life throws challenges at us, and we find ourselves floundering. To use an illustration from the prophet Isaiah, we walk "in darkness and [have] no light" (Isa. 50:10). And some trials seem, at least to us, to have no purpose. It is interesting that the Bible records God Himself saying as much to Satan: "You incited me against him to destroy him *without reason*"[1] (Job 2:3, emphasis added). Of course, nothing God does is "without reason" *for Him*. His actions are always purposeful. Nothing He does is random. But it sometimes appears to us as though God's actions are indiscriminate and haphazard. The trials seem pointless—so much so that we find ourselves thinking, "Does God *really* care?"[2]

Finding help in the midst of our trials is what this book is about. And the help that we have in mind is that offered in the second half of Isaiah. This is not the place to address the technical issues of whether there are, in fact, *two* or even *three* Isaiahs. Let me insist at once that I do not believe this hypothesis. Much Old Testament scholarship, however, having lost touch with the Bible's own self-attesting authority, has long since balked at Isaiah's ability to accurately predict events that came more than a century and a half after his death. Hence, there must be "another" Isaiah—someone who claimed to be Isaiah—who wrote during or even after the Babylonian exile. This "other" Isaiah supposedly gave accurate prophecies from a later historical vantage point, where the interjection of a sympathetic Persian king looked far more likely than it did in the eighth century BC. Conclusions suggesting two or even three "Isaiahs" are expressions of disbelief in the inerrancy of Scripture. Suffice it to say that I do not believe this hypothesis is necessary.

*Strength for the Weary* is not a commentary on the entirety of the second half of Isaiah. Instead, I have chosen some of the great texts from this magnificent portion of Scripture. The choice of texts was somewhat random; they are verses that have meant a great deal to me over the years and seem particularly poignant for the antagonistic culture in which we currently live. Here are some examples of these texts:

Comfort, comfort my people, says your God. (Isa. 40:1)

He gives power to the faint,
    and to him who has no might he increases strength. (Isa. 40:29)

I am the LORD, and there is no other,
    besides me there is no God. (Isa. 45:5)

Come, everyone who thirsts,
    come to the waters;
and he who has no money,
    come, buy and eat!
Come, buy wine and milk
    without money and without price. (Isa. 55:1)

For behold, I create new heavens
    and a new earth,
and the former things shall not be remembered
    or come into mind. (Isa. 65:17)

Texts such as these are powerful weapons against unbelief and fear. When we commit them to memory and employ them when Satan and his minions attack us, these passages of Scripture can help us walk tall and reflect the glory of the Lord.

*Strength for the Weary* is therefore designed to do what the title suggests: provide encouragement to weary pilgrims on their journey through this world of trial and sorrow.

Currently, you may find yourself in "green pastures" and "beside still waters," to cite the imagery of Psalm 23. If so, you may count yourself blessed indeed. But my guess is that if you have made it this far, you are in one of the other places mentioned in this psalm: "in the valley of the shadow of death" or "in the presence of [your] enemies." If so, Isaiah's timeless words of comfort are for you.

Three works on Isaiah by the late Alec Motyer are referenced in this book.[3] He "finished the race" in the summer of 2016, and a few days before the news of his home-calling arrived, I received a letter from him in the mail. I will always treasure it. Dr. Motyer was (and remains) the finest scholar on all things related to Isaiah, and consulting anyone else seemed superfluous.

These chapters formed part of a short series of sermons preached at First Presbyterian Church, Columbia, S.C., where I currently minister. These folks are very special indeed, and I am grateful to God for the honor of serving them. My sweet bride, Rosemary, is also part of my story. This year, we celebrated forty years of marriage. I cannot imagine life without her strength and support. There are no words sufficient to express my gratitude for her.

A dear friend, Dr. William (Bill) Bates, kindly agreed to proofread this manuscript, and I am greatly indebted to him for his invaluable insights. What errors remain are entirely mine.

Over the years, these great passages in Isaiah have done my soul much good. My prayer is that they will also help you to "be strengthened with power through his Spirit in your inner being, so that Christ may dwell in your hearts through faith" (Eph. 3:16b–17a).

—Derek W.H. Thomas
Christmas 2016

# 1

# STRENGTH FOR
# THE WEARY

He gives power to the faint,
  and to him who has no might he increases strength. (Isa. 40:29)

Playing hide-and-seek is a child's game. It is usually characterized by fun and laughter. Unless, that is, the stakes are raised and it becomes a sinister episode between God and me. All of a sudden, it is no longer a game, but a nightmare.

God has hidden Himself from me and I cannot find Him.

God has hidden Himself from me and doesn't want to be found.

"My way is hidden from the LORD." (Isa. 40:27)

"Has God forgotten me?" Have you ever asked that question?

Christians *do* experience such days more frequently than we might admit. Consider the following trio of passages:

Why, O Lord, do you stand far away? Why do you hide yourself in times of trouble? (Ps. 10:1)

Why do you hide your face? Why do you forget our affliction and oppression? (Ps. 44:24)

How long, O Lord? Will you hide yourself forever? (Ps. 89:46)

*God doesn't love me anymore.* Can believers really think this? Yes, they can. And do.

It is what the serpent (Satan) suggested to Adam and Eve in the garden of Eden—that "God doesn't love you as much as you think He does." In effect, Satan was saying, "If God *really* loved you, He wouldn't deprive you of this fruit."

And Adam and Eve believed the serpent more than they did the reassurances of God. The voice of the serpent drowned out the sound of God's voice. And in the silence, they wandered away.

Evidently, those to whom the prophet Isaiah spoke in the eighth century BC were facing the same danger. God seemed "hidden" from their eyes.

Finding God in difficult times is what this book is about. We will therefore almost exclusively confine ourselves to the second half of the book of Isaiah.[1] For here, too, in the period of Israel's history leading up to eventual exile in Babylon—a century and a half in their future—the prophet predicts that the Lord's people will experience a "dark night of the soul."

## 605, 597, AND 586 BC:
## THE DESTRUCTION OF JERUSALEM

Transporting us into this future exile, Isaiah imagines the Lord's people believing the same lie as Adam and Eve in the garden. "How can God love me if He has abandoned me and my family to life in exile?"

Imagine, then, the story.

Over a period of twenty years, Jerusalem witnessed its own complete demise. In 605 BC, the first wave of deportations took place. Young men, such as Daniel, were taken to Babylon. In 597 BC, men such as the prophet Ezekiel were taken into captivity. Then, in 586 BC, the city of Jerusalem was destroyed, its walls torn down, and the temple ransacked and demolished. Zedekiah, Judah's final king, had his eyes put out after the murder of his two sons. Watching his sons die was the last thing he saw, and he ended his days in a Babylonian prison.

Jerusalem was set ablaze.

War is often glamorized, but in reality, it is about death and destruction, rape and torture. Little wonder then, that God's people were reduced to spiritual darkness. Where is the Lord in this calamity? How could He possibly permit such things to occur?

"My way is hidden from the Lord."

"Is this how it's going to be from now on? Pointless, humdrum, without purpose or ambition?"

Locked in a dark cave of despair and gloom. Not so much "the best life now" but "the best life is somewhere in the past and it's never coming back."

Trapped. Betrayed. Forsaken. That is how many of the Lord's people felt.

"Stuff happens and it can't be undone. There's no hope for me now. There's no 'better future' out there. There's only this miserable existence."

This was a dark place, and some of God's children know its terrain all too well. They "[walk] in darkness and [have] no light" (Isa. 50:10). They lose their assurance of salvation.

And it is to Isaiah's description of spiritual darkness that the Westminster divines were drawn when describing the experience of the loss of assurance: "True believers may have the assurance of their salvation divers ways shaken, diminished, and intermitted . . . by God's withdrawing the light of His countenance, and suffering even such as fear Him to walk in darkness and to have no light."[2]

If Babylon's tyranny lay more than a century into the future, Assyria—in many ways, an even more savage and a greater military threat—was on Isaiah's doorstep. This is the concern of the first "half" of Isaiah's prophecy. It is time, then, for us to rehearse, very briefly, the message of the first half of Isaiah's prophecy.

## THE FLOODWATERS OF ASSYRIA

Isaiah's ministry covers a little more than half a century, from the 740s to the 680s BC, "the days of Uzziah, Jotham, Ahaz, and Hezekiah, kings of Judah" (Isa. 1:1). This provides the backdrop to the first thirty-nine chapters of the prophecy of Isaiah. The empire of Assyria was on the rise, and it had one thing on its mind: expansion.

With the accession of Tiglath-Pileser III (also known as Pul) in 745 BC, the glory days of Israel (in the north) and Judah (in the south) were numbered. In 722 BC, after a three-year siege, Samaria, the capital of the northern kingdom of Israel, fell to Shalmaneser (2 Kings 17:3–6). Israel, as a political and national entity, ceased to exist.

Isaiah's focus was the southern kingdom of Judah, with its capital, Jerusalem. Here, too, the remorseless Assyrian war machine made its presence felt. Isaiah warned in graphic terms of "waters of the River, mighty and many, the king of Assyria and all his glory. And it will rise over all its channels and go over all its banks, and it will sweep on into Judah, it will overflow and pass on, reaching even to the neck" (Isa. 8:7–8).

And in 701 BC, as recorded in vivid detail in Isaiah 36–37, Assyria's King Sennacherib attacked Jerusalem. The account is graphic and terrifying, for the Assyrian army far outnumbered the pitiful forces of Jerusalem. But the inhabitants of Jerusalem were miraculously delivered from the Assyrian threat. On the eve of an invasion that would surely overtake Jerusalem, 185,000 Assyrian soldiers were struck down (Isa. 37:36–37; cf. 2 Kings 19:35). God showed His mercy to His people.

On the horizon, however, another terror was ascending: Babylon. This mighty nation became the preoccupation of the second half of Isaiah, from chapter 40 onward. The events recorded here lay beyond Isaiah's lifetime. Isaiah was exercising his gift of prophecy.

## COMFORT

The comfort that resonates at the opening of chapter 40 is designed to bring relief to a people not yet born.

> Comfort, comfort my people, says your God.
> Speak tenderly to Jerusalem. (Isa. 40:1)

These words speak of a deliverance that is more than a century and a half away from Hezekiah, the prideful king with whom Isaiah deals in chapters 36–39.

In Hezekiah's time, Babylon was but a distant cloud on the horizon and seemingly no threat to Judah. When the king of Babylon, Merodach-baladan, made what looked like a state visit to Jerusalem, Hezekiah, blind to Babylonian ambition, was flattered. When Isaiah inquired as to what had been shown the Babylonian king, Hezekiah replied in effect, *everything!* All of Jerusalem's treasures and pitiful defense systems had been revealed. Isaiah's response was swift and solemn:

> Behold, the days are coming, when all that is in your house, and that which your fathers have stored up till this day, shall be carried to Babylon. Nothing shall be left, says the Lord. And some of your own sons, who will come from you, whom you will father, shall be taken away, and they shall be eunuchs in the palace of the king of Babylon. (Isa. 39:6–7)

The reference to "eunuchs" is all too clear: Hezekiah's future line would no longer produce sons. The succession of Judah's monarchy was heading to an ignominious end.

But that was in the future, for now at least, or so Hezekiah thought: "There will be peace and security in my days" (Isa. 39:8). How astonishingly self-centered and myopic. Alec Motyer's comments concerning this episode are perceptive: "Works have replaced faith, man has replaced God, and pride has replaced humility."[3]

And more than a century and a half later, during the Babylonian exile, God's people imagined that they were forsaken and forgotten. God was far away. Hope had forsaken them.

Who could blame them?

A similar gloom may descend on us in very different circumstances. When a husband or wife is suddenly taken away by death or walks out of a marriage for another; when the security of a job is threatened and we are thrown into the fog of an uncertain future; when relationships turn sour or dreams and aspirations are shattered, it may seem that God has forgotten us, too. And this is where the consolations of Isaiah 40 have timeless value. There is comfort here for *me* in *my* situation.

## THE BOOK OF CONSOLATION

The rabbis called Isaiah 40–66 "the Book of Consolation." Indeed, chapter 40 begins with the very familiar words set for the tenor voice in Handel's *Messiah:*

> Comfort ye, comfort ye my people, saith your God.
> Speak ye comfortably to Jerusalem, and cry unto her, that her warfare is accomplished, that her iniquity is pardoned. (Isa. 40:1–2, KJV)

These words occur at the beginning of a new chapter and a new section in Isaiah, but in the Dead Sea Scroll of Isaiah, these words continue from the final verse of what we call chapter 39 without any hint of a break.[4] From the doom of Isaiah's warning of Babylonian exile to the glorious words of triumphant release, without so much as a pause for breath! Glorious! God knows the end and the beginning. And when we find ourselves in the fog of despair, He knows the way out. He knows how this story will end because He has planned it and controls it.

For Isaiah's first readers, the need for consolation was urgent. If what Isaiah said concerning the exile were true—deportation to Babylon and the males of the royal family becoming eunuchs—then Isaiah's earlier prophetic promise of a coming King (chapters 9 and 11) sound like hot air. How can there be a future King (and kingdom) if there are no more heirs to the throne of Judah?

All the more wonderful, then, the promise God makes:

> For to us a child is born,
>> to us a son is given;
> and the government shall be upon his shoulder,
>> and his name shall be called
> Wonderful Counselor, Mighty God,
>> Everlasting Father, Prince of Peace.
> Of the increase of his government and of peace
>> there will be no end,
> on the throne of David and over his kingdom,
>> to establish it and to uphold it. (Isa. 9:6–7)

8

There shall come forth a shoot from the stump of Jesse,
and a branch from his roots shall bear fruit.
And the Spirit of the LORD shall rest upon him,
the Spirit of wisdom and understanding,
the Spirit of counsel and might,
the Spirit of knowledge and the fear of the LORD. . . .
and he shall strike the earth with the rod of his mouth,
and with the breath of his lips he shall kill the wicked.
(Isa. 11:1–4)

How could any of this come to pass if what Isaiah told Hezekiah were true? The answer, of course, is that a King of a very different kind was coming: King *Jesus*!

No wonder the prophet launches into a word of consolation so abruptly, with a trio of voices:

A voice cries. . . . A voice says, "Cry!" . . . lift up your voice. . . .
(Isa. 40:3, 6, 9)

And what is that word? An *imperative*—"comfort my people." God commands that His people be comforted. Our comfort, our well-being in the deepest and grandest of senses, lies as a burden upon His heart.

What kind of God is the God of Israel, the God of Judah—*our* God? Answer: He is a God who is eager for us to find peace and consolation amid the trials and hardships of life. A peacemaker. A caregiver.

POWER FOR THE FAINT

God has *not* forgotten them, nor has He forgotten us.

> He gives power to the faint,
>> and to him who has no might he increases strength.
> Even youths shall faint and be weary,
>> and young men shall fall exhausted;
> but they who wait for the LORD shall renew their strength;
>> they shall mount up with wings like eagles;
> they shall run and not be weary;
>> they shall walk and not faint. (Isa. 40:29–31)

Fainting souls soaring like eagles. Weary feet running. Faith revived.

> Why do you say, O Jacob,
>> and speak, O Israel,
> "My way is hidden from the LORD,
>> and my right is disregarded by my God"? (Isa. 40:27)

God issues a challenge: the people of Israel are not to think of themselves any longer like Jacob, hobbling after his encounter with God. They are Israel—renewed in strength and vision and purpose (cf. Gen. 32:22–32).

God challenges unbelief and doubt for being the withering cancer that it is.

Few challenged unbelief with greater boldness than Martin Luther. Writing in 1530, Luther chided his friend Philip Melanchthon for his doubting:

I too am sometimes downcast, but not all the time. It is your philosophy that is tormenting you, not your theology. . . . What good do you expect to accomplish by these vain worries of yours? What can the devil do more than slay us? Yes, what? I beg you, who are so pugnacious in everything else, fight against yourself, your own worst enemy, for you furnish Satan with too many weapons against yourself. Christ died for our sins. He will not die again for truth and justice, but will live and reign. If this be true, and if he reigns, why should you be afraid for the truth? Perhaps you are afraid that it will be destroyed by God's wrath. Even if we ourselves should be destroyed, let it not be by our own hands. He who is our Father will also be the Father of our children.[5]

## YOUR GOD IS TOO SMALL

*Your God Is Too Small* is the title of the book written by J.B. Phillips,[6] and in some ways, the expression reflects the problems that lay behind the plaintive cry of abandonment felt by Judah's exiles during the sixth century BC.

Perhaps they thought that their circumstances were too complicated for God to unravel and fix. What they needed, therefore, was a reminder of God's sovereignty and power.

Perhaps a subtler thought occurred to them: the suspicion that they were unworthy of God's attention. How can the infinite God of heaven and earth be concerned with "little ol' me"? My issues seem so trivial by comparison:

And the justice due me escapes the notice of my God? (Isa. 40:27, NASB)

God seems to be dismissing me. My prayers are not answered but ignored and disregarded. It feels unjust, unfair, and unwarranted.

And it is this that the sixteenth-century Reformer Martin Luther was getting at when he made the accusation of Erasmus, "Your thoughts of God are too human."[7]

Unbelief is a withering sickness that ultimately destroys faith. And what is the remedy? *Waiting* on the Lord:

> They who *wait for the LORD* shall renew their strength. (Isa. 40:31, emphasis added)

There are many kinds of waiting.

There is the "I am waiting for my spouse, sitting in the car, the engine running, and he/she is nowhere in sight" kind of waiting. It is impatient, petulant, rude.

Then there is the "dog lying by the front door, eyes drooping, body language indicating little or no hope that the master is returning anytime soon" kind of waiting. It is pitiful and sad.

There is also the "lover, listening to the words of a beloved partner, eyes wide open, gesturing surprise, amusement, love, and thankfulness, waiting for the next word to come forth." It is anticipatory and congratulatory.

What kind of waiting is in view here? The word for "wait" in the passage cited above is sometimes translated in the ESV text as "hope" (Ps. 62:5; Prov. 11:7) and sometimes "expectation" (Prov. 10:28; 11:23). In this passage, waiting involves looking away from ourselves and our troubles and looking to the Lord in faith and with expectation. And not just *looking*, but *expecting . . . trusting . . . believing*. Taking a long, hard look at who God is: His character, His being, His Word, His promise, His commitment, His covenant, His unchanging determination to do what He said He would do.

> Have you not known? Have you not heard?
> The LORD is the everlasting God,
>     the Creator of the ends of the earth.
> He does not faint or grow weary;
>     his understanding is unsearchable. (Isa. 40:28)

Isaiah's prescription for this withering sickness of unbelief is a dose of God's magnificent majesty, power, and glory. The promises of God are guaranteed by *who* and *what* He is. He is the Creator and Sustainer of the world and His people.

A single verse encapsulates what Isaiah elaborates on throughout the chapter. Exploring the character of God, Isaiah seems to be saying, "Look at Him! Take a long, hard look at Him!"

And what will we see if we do so?

- The Lord is *everlasting*—in the sense that He is eternal, outside the fluctuating contours of time and space. The same yesterday, today, and forever, because these expressions of time are perspectives that are all too human and creaturely. God is "outside" and "above" all these limiting dimensions. He alone has being in Himself (what theologians call "aseity"). The problem with man-made gods—"idols," to give them their proper name (Isa. 40:19)—is just that: they are man-made. These artifacts may require the skill of craftsmen, but it is a craft of *men* nevertheless. The problem with human gods is that they do not actually exist. They have "being" only in the fertile imagination of sinful minds and hearts.

- The Lord is *omnipresent* in the sense that He created "the ends of the earth" and no part of it is a mystery to Him. There are no boundaries beyond which He cannot pass. No dropped calls or dead zones where our voices cannot be heard or His voice cannot get through.

- The Lord is *omnipotent*. He is the Creator who spoke and the universe came into being (Gen. 1:1). He calls out the stars each night and introduces them by name (Isa. 40:26). He does not tire or grow weary. His strength is infinite. He does not need to rest or sleep. He preserves in the face of all opposition. Strong young men grow weary, but the Lord does not (Isa. 40:30).[8] And the Lord knows and understands this and compensates by supplying His people with His strength.

- The Lord is *great*. So vast is the Lord that the universe and all it contains appears as "nothing . . . less than nothing and emptiness" (Isa. 40:17).[9] All earthly pretenders (Assyrian, Babylonian, Persian, Greek, and Roman) are but as "grasshoppers" (Isa. 40:22) in comparison to the Almighty.

- The Lord is *wise* in the sense that He is omniscient and knows what to do with this knowledge to accomplish His good purposes. His knowledge and understanding are so vast that they are unsearchable to us. He is incomprehensible, and as Job did when he discovered this truth, we should put our hands to our mouths and be silent.[10]

In one verse, Isaiah provides us with a magnificent portrait of God. As Motyer summarizes, "In one way or another the four-fold Old Testament doctrine of God the Creator is represented here: he originates everything, maintains everything in existence, controls everything in operation, and directs everything to the end that he appoints."[11]

Open your eyes and take a good, long, hard look at God:

Lift up your eyes and see. (Isa. 40:26)

There is no one like our God.

To whom will you compare me? (Isa. 40:25)

God is in a category all His own. And knowing this brings strength and vitality.

It is not strength in ourselves that is encouraged here but strength *in Him*—in the sovereign, all-powerful, all-wise, all-sustaining, never-tiring God.

Are you weary? Losing faith in God's promises? Tired in the heat of the battle? Overwhelmed by the opposition?

Then what you need is a fresh glimpse of the majesty of God.

Sometimes, we cannot see what is right before us and above us.

In C.S. Lewis' *The Last Battle*, there is a wonderful description of how we can be in two different worlds *at the same time.*

In one world, there is Tirian and Peter and Lucy and Jill, friends of Aslan. And there is summer and blue skies. In another world, there is a company of dwarves, and all they see is a dark and dirty stable:

> Instantly a glorious feast appeared on the Dwarfs' knees: pies and tongues and pigeons and trifles and ices, and each Dwarf had a goblet of good wine in his right hand. But it wasn't much use. They began eating and drinking greedily enough, but it was clear that they couldn't taste it properly. They thought they were eating and drinking only the sort of things you might find in a stable. One said he was trying to eat hay and another said he had a bit of an old turnip and a third said he'd found a raw cabbage leaf. And they raised golden goblets of rich red wine to their lips and said "Ugh! Fancy drinking dirty water out of a trough that a donkey's been at! Never thought we'd come to this." . . . "You see," said Aslan, "They will not let us help them. They have chosen cunning instead of belief. Their prison is only in their own minds, yet they are in that prison; and so afraid of being taken in that they cannot be taken out."[12]

Which world are you in right now?

# 2

# WHO RULES THE WORLD?

"You are my witnesses," declares the LORD,
    "and my servant whom I have chosen,
that you may know and believe me
    and understand that I am he.
Before me no god was formed,
    nor shall there be any after me.
I, I am the LORD,
    and besides me there is no savior." (Isa. 43:10–11)

*Why?*

It is a question we ask when difficult circumstances arise. Rarely is there a satisfying answer, even for Christians.

For my thoughts are not your thoughts, neither are your ways my ways, declares the LORD. (Isa. 55:8)

Sometimes the question turns inward—*Why me?*

This, too, is understandable. We want answers to personal questions. Why has my life turned upside down? And, like Job, we face the silence of unanswered questions only to be left with another question: *Who?* For in the midst of the pain and heartache is our inscrutable, unchangeable, sovereign Lord. And when we discover Him, and fall into His arms, there is a peace that surpasses all understanding (Phil. 4:7).

It is the *Who?* question, rather than the *Why?* question, that occupies the section of Isaiah from 42:18 through 43:21.

> Who gave up Jacob to the looter, and Israel to the plunderers?
> (Isa. 42:24)

Some background is needed to understand the source of the question.

## BABYLON

The prophet foresees Israel's captivity in Babylon (Isa. 43:14). They will be a people plundered and looted, trapped in holes and prisons (Isa. 42:22). There will be none to rescue. And Isaiah imagines the plaintive cry, "Who did this to Israel?" The answer was clear.

> Was it not the LORD, against whom we have sinned,
>     in whose ways they would not walk,
>     and whose law they would not obey? (Isa. 42:24)

Israel had only themselves to blame. The reason for their captivity was their sins and transgressions (Isa. 42:24; 43:25). Babylon was their punishment.

Earlier, the prophet described how Israel would be a light to the nations (Isa. 42:6). The end of the earth would sing to the Lord a new song (Isa. 42:10). The nations were blind and deaf (Isa. 42:18).[1] But Israel, too, was blind—"Who is blind but my servant, or deaf as my messenger whom I send?" (Isa. 42:9).[2]

Can the blind (Israel) lead the blind (the nations)? The answer must be no. How can this dilemma be solved? The solution lies in the rise of another servant:

> Behold my servant, whom I uphold,
>> my chosen, in whom my soul delights;
> I have put my Spirit upon him;
>> he will bring forth justice to the nations.
> He will not cry aloud or lift up his voice,
>> or make it heard in the street;
> a bruised reed he will not break,
>> and a faintly burning wick he will not quench;
> he will faithfully bring forth justice.
> He will not grow faint or be discouraged
> till he has established justice in the earth;
>> and the coastlands wait for his law. (Isa. 42:1–4)

This servant is, of course, Jesus. More will be said later about how Isaiah foretells the coming of the Messiah. For now, we remain engulfed in a description of Israel's waywardness and rebellion—the reason why they (and we) need a Messiah, a Savior.

Israel had been careless about God's works and ways. Calling her by the masculine "he" (as a servant-leader might be depicted), the prophet describes how Israel was privileged to see and hear many things that the gentile nations do not see or acknowledge. However, Israel remained willfully blind and deaf despite her privileges:

> He sees many things, but does not observe them;
>> his ears are open, but he does not hear. (Isa. 42:20)

A list of failures follow: willful blindness, spiritual insensitivity, culpable deafness, and flagrant disobedience (Isa. 42:18–25). In particular, Isaiah singles out the fact that Israel had failed to display that for which she had been created: "whom I created for my glory" (Isa. 43:7).

Man's chief end is to glorify God and to enjoy Him forever. So says the answer to the first question of the Westminster Shorter Catechism. This answer reflects something the Apostle Paul wrote when he, like Isaiah, analyzed the essential nature of man's sinfulness: "All have sinned and fall short of the glory of God" (Rom. 3:23).

The essence of sin is to curve in upon ourselves and fail to reflect the glory of God—the image given to us at creation (cf. Gen. 1:26–27).

By keeping God's law, we reflect something of God's glory. Our holiness is meant to mirror God's holiness—the holiness of the One whom Isaiah on twenty-five occasions calls "the Holy One of Israel" (Isa. 43:3; cf. 1:4). Like all of Adam's progeny by nature, Israel was created to give praise to God. Yet Israel flouted God's law and failed to give Him the glory due His name.

What is shocking is that Isaiah is describing God's covenant people. Despite all the privileges that grace affords, there was still abject failure and betrayal. It was a wonder that the Lord did not abandon them.

He did not abandon them, but He did *chastise* them.

It is vital that we appreciate the difference between abandonment and chastisement.

There are consequences to behavior, especially Christian behavior. These consequences follow *because* we are Christians.

> My son, do not regard lightly the discipline of the Lord,
>> nor be weary when reproved by him.
> For the Lord disciplines the one he loves,
>> and chastises every son whom he receives. (Heb. 12:5–6, citing Prov. 3:11–12)

> So he poured on him the heat of his anger
>> and the might of battle;
> it set him on fire all around, but he did not understand;
>> it burned him up, but he did not take it to heart. (Isa. 42:25)

The Puritan preacher and theologian Stephen Charnock once wrote, "We often learn more of God under the rod that strikes us, than under the staff that comforts us."[3]

Not every trial is a form of chastisement. Job's suffering, for example, came through no particular fault of his own. Three times we are told—by God Himself—of Job's innocence (Job 1:1, 8; 2:3).

A similar example appears with the man Jesus encountered who was blind from birth. Jesus' disciples assumed immediately that the cause of the man's suffering was due either to himself or to his parents, but Jesus responded, "It was not that this man sinned, or his parents, but that the works of God might be displayed in him" (John 9:3). Whatever the reason for the man's suffering, it lay outside of any consideration of the blind man's sin.

In Isaiah, things are different. The trial is God's reprimand, and His people would pass through fire.

> When you walk through fire you shall not be burned,
>     and the flame shall not consume you. (Isa. 43:2)

And though we may want to jump immediately to the reassurance (that Israel would not be consumed), we first need to assimilate the reality of the trial and its cause.

The Lord sends fire, but He does not abandon His covenant people or wipe them out. Instead, He intends to renew and restore and revive His people.

This is the principal lesson of this passage. God renews a people who have lost their sense of purpose. He may have given up Israel to the plunderers (Babylon), but He will restore them and much more besides. The covenant Lord has a plan that He intends to fulfill. And there is no stopping God when He determines to do something: "I work, and who can turn it back?" (Isa. 43:13).

## A GOD LIKE NO OTHER

What kind of God does the prophet proclaim in Isaiah 42:18–43:21? What must God be like if He promises to restore and renew despite the abject failure of His people? What kind of God is our covenant Lord? The answer is that He is like no other!

> I, I am the LORD,
>> and besides me there is no savior. (Isa. 43:11)

In a series of statements that open chapter 43, a sixfold depiction of God's glory emerges.

First, God is the *Creator*. Using two distinct words, both found in the carefully constructed narrative of creation in Genesis 1 and 2, Isaiah describes God as having "created" and "formed" Jacob/Israel:

> But now thus says the LORD,
> he who created you, O Jacob,
>> he who formed you, O Israel. (Isa. 43:1)

The first word, "created" (*bara*), usually refers to the creation of something *new*. It does not necessarily imply that the creative result was *ex nihilo*, out of nothing. Genesis 2:7 tells us that man was not created (*bara*) *ex nihilo* but from "the dust of the earth."

The second word, "formed" (*yatsar*[4]), can be rendered "to knead." Later in Isaiah, a form of this word is translated "potter"[5] and implies the use of preexisting material. The emphasis is on sovereignty. In "forming" Adam, God used "the dust of the ground" *and* breathed into him the breath of life. In a sense, God "kissed" Adam into life (Gen. 2:7).

Later, a third word is employed—"made" (*yaas*).[6] This word suggests the labor of God in "giving perfect expression to his creative designs, bringing the acts of creation to their intended concrete expression."[7]

Like Adam, Israel is the product of God's sovereign determination and skill. God's people are no accident. Thought, premeditation, and divine dexterity are involved in Israel's creation. Like Adam, Israel owes allegiance, obedience, and reciprocal affection. She is not her own creator. She owes her existence and her salvation to the Lord.

Ideas have consequences. The blurring and sometimes complete loss of the doctrine of creation in our time affects the way we understand our nature and function as human beings. Creation is a reminder that the relationship we have with God is not that of equals. We owe our existence to Him, and we are essentially subordinate. Even in the most intimate of relationships of our redeemed status—that of adopted sons—we are still creatures. Though saved and adopted creatures, we are creatures nevertheless. We exist to serve the Lord, and we are redeemed to serve the Lord.

Second, he is our *Redeemer*: "I have redeemed you" (Isa. 43:1). He has taken the role of Boaz and acted as our Kinsman-Redeemer, our next-of-kin with all the legal and family obligations this relationship entails. Our debt became His. He paid in full what we, or Israel, could not pay. He fulfilled what the law required on our behalf.[8] It is a glorious truth that the Lord will pay whatever it takes to ransom His people from captivity, even His own Son.

> Redeemed, how I love to proclaim it!
> Redeemed by the blood of the Lamb;
> Redeemed through His infinite mercy,
> His child and forever I am.
>
> Redeemed, redeemed,
> Redeemed by the blood of the Lamb;
> Redeemed, redeemed,
> His child and forever I am.[9]

Third, God is our *Preserver*. Purchase implies ownership. "You are mine," God says. And, underlying the intimacy of this relationship, we are on first-name terms: "I have called you by name" (Isa. 43:1). God knows my name, and He knows yours. His love ensures that we will come to no ultimate harm. We may be asked to pass through the waters and the rivers, and even fire and flame, but they will not overwhelm or consume (Isa. 43:2). He preserves His people through the trial. We may not be spared *from* the trial, but we will be spared *through* the trial. This is what our redemption means: we are *His*.

Fourth, God is *loving*. In words of inexpressible beauty and intimacy, God tells Israel,

> You are precious in my eyes,
> and honored, and I love you. . . . (Isa. 43:4)

We are precious to Him and loved by Him.

God calls us by name, introducing us to *His* name: "For I am the Lord your God" (Isa. 43:3).

God's personal name is YHWH or Yahweh (usually rendered in English Bibles as "Lord"). He revealed Himself to Moses in Exodus 3 by the name "I am who I am," (Ex. 3:14), later shortened to "I am." In that context, His name was closely associated with His promise and covenant. In effect, God was saying, "I am the God who made covenant with your fathers and I will be a God who keeps it with you."

> "The Lord, the God of your fathers, the God of Abraham, the God of Isaac, and the God of Jacob, has sent me to you." This is my name forever, and thus I am to be remembered throughout all generations. (Ex. 3:15)

We live in a generation where esteem means a great deal. Nothing spells "esteem" more than the knowledge that we are loved. Loved by another. Loved by God. A love that will not let us go.

Fifth, God is a *Gatherer and Rescuer*. He will gather from east and west. Wherever we are, He will find us. With more than the future captivity in Babylon in mind, God says:

> Fear not, for I am with you;
>     I will bring your offspring from the east,
>     and from the west I will gather you.
> I will say to the north, Give up,
>     and to the south, Do not withhold;

bring my sons from afar
and my daughters from the end of the earth. (Isa. 43:5–6)

The prophet seems to be looking beyond Babylon and into a future—*our* present and *our* future. "I will find you," God seems to be saying, "wherever you are."

Set in the upper New York wilderness in 1757, *The Last of the Mohicans* tells the story of the transport of the two daughters of Colonel Munro, Alice and Cora, to a safe destination at Fort William Henry. Among others, including Mohican scouts, is Nathaniel ("Natty Bumpo," played by Daniel Day-Lewis in the 1992 film). In a massacre that ensues following an attack by Huron warriors, Nathaniel sees no way out but to escape and leave Cora to the mercy of the Hurons. "I will find you," Nathaniel says to her before diving through the waterfall, "no matter how long it takes, no matter how far. I will find you."

Not one will be lost in the gathering of God's people. "I will find you," God says. He knows each of us by name. He protects each one individually.

The one lost in the darkness of depression.

The one trapped in a loveless and abusive marriage.

The one tempted and allured by false gods with false promises.

There is no "left behind" narrative in the electing and saving purposes of God. Importantly, this promise is made to the redeemed only. Like a shepherd who braves wind and storm to find the lost sheep, God will leave the "ninety-nine in the open country, and go after the one that is lost, until he has found it" (Luke 15:4).

Sixth, God is *glorious* and is determined to get all the glory for Himself. As we saw earlier in this chapter, He formed us to that end: "whom I created for my glory" (Isa. 43:7). In a courtroom drama, Isaiah ushers Israel into an examination of their myopic failure (Isa. 43:8–13). Witnesses are summoned and accusations made. Their unseeing eyes and deaf ears are testimonies to the fact that they have failed to appreciate the sole reason for their existence: to give glory to God. Man's dalliance with idols is evidence of this shortsightedness:

> "Before me no god was formed,
>> nor shall there be any after me.
> I, I am the LORD,
>> and besides me there is no savior.
> I declared and saved and proclaimed,
>> when there was no strange god among you;
>> and you are my witnesses," declares the LORD, "and I am God."
> (Isa. 43:10–12)

These "strange gods" are man's greatest crimes, and they are palpably incapable of delivering Israel from their trials. Yahweh alone is God, and Yahweh alone can deliver.

## THE UNIQUENESS OF GOD

The three cultural giants of the nineteenth century—Ludwig Feuerbach, Sigmund Freud, and Friedrich Nietzsche—insisted that mankind is fueled by a propensity to idolatry. Of course, in their eyes, Christianity is an example of such idol worship. But they were right in pointing to this human weakness and failure. Calvin said the same when he wrote in his *Institutes of the Christian Religion* that the human mind is a perpetual factory of idols.[10]

An idol is something or someone inflated to function as God. Sometimes conservative Christians are little better at identifying idols than modern secular individuals.

Yet the prohibition is clear.

You shall have no other gods before me. (Ex. 20:3)

Little children, keep yourselves from idols. (1 John 5:21)

Isaiah will return to this theme again in chapter 45, speaking of those who carry gods around, praying to those that have no power to save (Isa. 45:20).

Ancient idols required the sacrifice of a life. Make no mistake: modern idols do, too. Idols want all of you. They promise everything and deliver nothing. We sacrifice to them, and they in turn manipulate and control. Idols are abusive and tyrannical. They cheat like the characters in a trashy daytime soap opera.

Not only that, they are powerless to save, heal, or restore. They offer hope and a purpose but return only disappointment and guilt. Like the One Ring, so captivatingly referred to as "the Precious" in J.R.R. Tolkien's *The Lord of the Rings*, idols allure and beckon only to return total, uncompromising evil.

## THE ATTRACTION OF IDOLS

We may find it hard to believe that Israel would be so allured by man-made objects so as to displace the Lord who had saved them. But the truth is, we give our allegiance to idols, too. We sacrifice to them. We believe they will bring us true and lasting purpose. They go by different names: money, power, houses, ambition, sports, or leisure.

As the antidote to this idolatry, Isaiah called upon God's people to consider the Lord. He alone offers something better and surer—a new thing:

> Behold, I am doing a new thing;
>> now it springs forth, do you not perceive it?
> I will make a way in the wilderness
>> and rivers in the desert.
> The wild beasts will honor me,
>> the jackals and the ostriches,
> for I give water in the wilderness,
>> rivers in the desert,
> to give drink to my chosen people,
>> the people whom I formed for myself
> that they might declare my praise. (Isa. 43:19–21)

We will return later to examine this "new thing," for the prophet will speak of it many times. A bright and shining future that bursts the boundaries of our thinking. An environment where peace and fulfillment in a new creation will emerge and all our parameters will be challenged:

"The wolf and the lamb shall graze together;
    the lion shall eat straw like the ox,
    and dust shall be the serpent's food.
They shall not hurt or destroy
    in all my holy mountain,"
    says the LORD. (Isa. 65:25)

Open your eyes and see. And believe!

Fear not, I am with thee; oh, be not dismayed,
For I am thy God and will still give thee aid.
I'll strengthen thee, help thee, and cause thee to stand,
Upheld by my righteous, upheld by my righteous,
Upheld by my righteous, omnipotent hand.

When through the deep waters I call thee to go,
The rivers of sorrow shall not thee o'erflow,
For I will be with thee, thy troubles to bless,
And sanctify to thee, and sanctify to thee,
And sanctify to thee thy deepest distress.[11]

# 3

# I AM THE
# ONLY GOD THERE IS

Turn to me and be saved,
>   all the ends of the earth!
>   For I am God, and there is no other. (Isa. 45:22)

I am God, and there is no other;
>   I am God, and there is none like me. (Isa. 46:9)

Predictive prophecy is the ability to pinpoint with infallible accuracy an event that will occur long after the prophet has died. Isaiah made a number of these prophecies:

- A virgin will conceive and bear a son (Isa. 7:14).
- The Messiah's work will begin in Galilee (Isa. 9:1–7).
- Through the Messiah's ministry, the blind will see and the deaf will hear (Isa. 35:1–6).

And, amazingly, Isaiah predicted the rise and fall of Babylon, along with the specific name of a future Persian conqueror/deliverer: Cyrus.[1]

## A DELIVERER

Chapters 42–48 of Isaiah tell us how God would deal with His people's desperate condition. This condition had both political (the exile) and spiritual (idolatry) dimensions. God would raise up a servant who would be a covenant for the people, a light for the nations (Isa. 42:1, 6). One might have expected the task of being a light for the nations to be given to the covenant people themselves, but they were disqualified. They were both deaf and blind (Isa. 42:19).

Two sections follow this announcement of the coming servant:

- The first exposes Judah's *political* need and her stupidity in looking to idols for help (Isa. 42:18–43:21). The result was their captivity: they would be a people plundered and looted (Isa. 42:22). The Lord was both able and willing to save them. Indeed, the section ends with a vision of a glorious future in which there will be "water in the wilderness, rivers in the desert" (Isa. 43:20).
- The second section exposes Judah's *spiritual* need (Isa. 43:22–44:23). In this section, God expresses their need, elaborates on His willingness and power to save, and ends with an equally glorious vision of the future in which

the earth, mountain, forest, and trees break forth into singing (Isa. 44:23).

According to Isaiah's prophecy, deliverance would come—
politically and spiritually. But *how* would this deliverance be
achieved? And *who* would this servant figure be, if not God's covenant people? The answer is as surprising now as it must have
been then: a Persian king named Cyrus.

> Thus says the LORD to his anointed, to Cyrus,
> > whose right hand I have grasped,
> to subdue nations before him
> > and to loose the belts of kings,
> to open doors before him
> > that gates may not be closed:
> "I will go before you
> > and level the exalted places,
> I will break in pieces the doors of bronze
> > and cut through the bars of iron,
> I will give you the treasures of darkness
> > and the hoards in secret places,
> that you may know that it is I, the LORD,
> > the God of Israel, who call you by your name." (Isa. 45:1–3)[2]

Cyrus did indeed issue a decree permitting the Jews to return
from Babylon to rebuild the temple in Jerusalem; it is a matter of
biblical and historical record. The book of Ezra begins with the
words, "In the first year of Cyrus king of Persia . . ." (Ezra 1:1).

We also have verification from Cyrus himself in the so-called Cyrus Cylinder. Discovered in the ruins of ancient Babylon in 1879, it contains a record of how exiled nations were ordered to return home, mimicking the Hebrew of Ezra 1:2–4 and the Aramaic of Ezra 6:2–5.[3]

PROPHECY

Two fundamental problems arise in connection with Cyrus. First, this event was two hundred years in the future. Second, Cyrus was a pagan king.

The first problem—the issue of timing—is a simple matter of asking, "Do you believe in the supernatural?" Is it possible for God to superintend the human thought process in such a way that what human prophets speak and write is the Word of God— the infallible, inerrant Word of God? For that *is* the claim the New Testament writers make when they speak of Old Testament authors of Scripture:

No prophecy was ever produced by the will of man, but men spoke from God as they were carried along by the Holy Spirit. (2 Peter 1:21)

All Scripture is breathed out by God. (2 Tim. 3:16)

The claim that Peter and Paul make in these verses is quite simply this: when the Bible speaks, God speaks. It is not just that God can be heard "in" Scripture—somewhere, somehow—but that Scripture *is* God's Word. Its verbs, nouns, adjectives, prepositions—each iota and dot—are God's Word.[4]

To be clear, Isaiah wrote this prophecy in the failing days of King Hezekiah, almost two centuries *before* the rise of Cyrus, king of Persia. How was this kind of forecasting possible?

For some, predictive prophecy of this kind is unbelievable, and thus some other explanation must be given. Examples of this obduracy include:

- The specific name "Cyrus" was written into the text at a later period.
- The section of Isaiah incorporating chapters 40–55 belongs to another (later) era and was written by a "different" Isaiah (a *deutero*-Isaiah), one who lived in the Babylonian exile and could discern that Cyrus just might be able to pull off a Persian overthrow of Babylon.

Such explanations arise because of a bias against the notion of predictive prophecy. It is a disbelief in the ability of the Holy Spirit to inform men such as Isaiah of future events. It is, in short, a form of anti-supernaturalism.

The Scottish skeptic David Hume outlines the argument against supernaturalism this way:

- Miracles are violations of natural laws.
- Natural laws are immutable.
- It is impossible to violate immutable laws.
- Therefore, miracles are impossible.

When asked if Christians *must* accept the possibility of miracles, C.S. Lewis wrote: "But if we admit God, must we admit Miracle? Indeed, indeed, you have no security against it. That is the bargain."[5]

What a thing of marvel the Bible is! We can trust its every word. As Kevin DeYoung writes: "Ultimately we believe the Bible because we believe in the power and wisdom and goodness and truthfulness of the God whose authority and veracity cannot be separated from the Bible. We trust the Bible because it is God's Bible. And God being God, we have every reason to take Him at his word."[6]

## A PAGAN KING

The fact that Cyrus was a pagan is a little more difficult, especially since Isaiah records God saying of Cyrus, he is My "shepherd" (Isa. 44:28) and My "anointed" (Isa. 45:1).

Both terms are rich in meaning and significance. In the Greek translation of Isaiah (the Septuagint), "anointed" is rendered *christos*. Cyrus the *Messiah* (the Hebrew word), the "Christ" figure.

Really? Can a pagan king be called *Messiah*?

Both "shepherd" and "anointed" were titles for the royal line of David. Thus, Davidic kings were called "shepherds" (Isa. 56:11). Could a Persian king be in the same league as a successor to David? More difficult still is the designation of Cyrus as Messiah. The psalmist pleaded David's status as Messiah in one of the Psalms of Ascents:

For the sake of your servant David,
do not turn away the face of your anointed one. (Ps. 132:10)

How could a pagan king be Judah's messianic deliverer?

Here the prophet Isaiah is preoccupied with the expectation of a coming deliverer, a Messiah figure. And for now, at least, this Messiah is not Jesus.

> Behold, a king will reign in righteousness,
>     and princes will rule in justice. (Isa. 32:1)

This king is Cyrus the Persian.

## THE GOOD, THE BAD, AND THE UGLY

Several things become clear in the prophecy concerning Cyrus.

First, God is sovereign, and He can employ whomever He likes to accomplish His purposes. What Cyrus accomplished is breathtaking:

- Subdued nations (Isa. 45:1).
- Opened doors of opportunity (Isa. 45:1).
- Removed all obstacles ("exalted places") (Isa. 45:2).
- Destroyed all resistance and opposition ("doors of bronze" and "bars of iron") (Isa. 45:2).
- Obtained "treasures" (Isa. 45:3).

And Cyrus accomplished these things because God declared, "I am the LORD, who does all these things" (Isa. 45:7). He is the potter and we have no right to complain about the shape of the pot He makes (Isa. 45:9).

Things happen and events occur because they are the fulfillment of God's plan and purpose. He is in charge of history. This is a statement of providence in its most comprehensive form. It includes light and darkness, prosperity and disaster:

I form light and create darkness;
I make well-being and create calamity;
I am the LORD, who does all these things. (Isa. 45:7)

The rise and fall of kings is in the hands of the Lord. Whatever the immediate or ultimate purpose might be, it is God who controls the course of world events. Presidents, dictators, kings, and queens—all are under the control of God.

And if this true, what should our response be?

- If God has plans for the future, we shouldn't complain about the present. If we don't like what He is doing in the present, it's because He hasn't yet finished. The present is on its way to the future, and every part of it is under His control.
- If God has plans for the future, there isn't a detail that is too "small" for him. To bring about an event of this kind (the rise of King Cyrus and the deliverance of God's people from captivity), a million things need to occur. And every one of them will occur because if they do not, the future cannot be certain.

This means that the little things are in His control, too. I call them "little things" because in comparison to the prophecy concerning Cyrus, they are little. But perhaps they are not little to us, especially when they involve heartache and hard questions:

- Why did my spouse get cancer?
- Why did I lose my job?
- Will my son come home from the war?
- Will I ever get pregnant and have children of my own?
- Can I find joy again?

These are big questions to those who ask them. But in the grand scheme of redemptive history, they are small questions. Most importantly, they are never ultimately *uncertain* questions. They may be uncertain to us, but they are not to God.

The Swiss Reformer Huldrych Zwingli defined providence this way: "All things are so done and disposed of by the providence of God that nothing takes place without his will or command."[7] He based this view largely on Jesus' observation of sparrows falling to the ground, adding that "not one of them will fall to the ground apart from [the will of] your Father" (Matt. 10:29).

Not only that, there is always a purpose behind what is happening, even if we cannot see it. It is the purpose of God. What is God's purpose in the shaping of history? This can be a very difficult ethical question. Is God to blame for the evil acts of despots (Idi Amin, Pol Pot, Adolf Hitler)? No, He is not. His governance is not deterministic. Evil rulers are responsible for their actions.

But perhaps we can ask a different question. What was God's intent in raising up Cyrus the way He did? Here is Isaiah's answer:

That you may know that it is I, the LORD,
>the God of Israel, who call you by your name. (Isa. 45:3)

I call you by your name,
>I name you, though you do not know me. (Isa. 45:4)

## GOD MOVES IN MYSTERIOUS WAYS

Did Cyrus acknowledge the God of Israel as his Lord? There is no evidence at all that he did.

It was God's will that the pagan king became Israel's Messiah-figure, the Lord's "anointed." And yet, in another sense, it evidently was not God's will that Cyrus was what he was. How can this be?

It is here that theologians engage in a little subterfuge. Or at least, it appears that way at first sight. They insist that we differentiate between the will of God's "events" and the will of God's "command."[8] One is always done. The other is often frustrated. In one sense, everything happens because God has willed it to happen. There are no "black holes" in God's providence. This includes sin and evil. But clearly, in another sense, it is not God's will that we sin.

But let's think of this another way. Did Cyrus himself acknowledge God's hand in his life? Absolutely! Knowing as he did that his name had been uttered a century and a half before his birth by a prophet from Jerusalem, he gave credit to the Lord:

Thus says Cyrus king of Persia: The LORD, the God of heaven, has given me all the kingdoms of the earth, and he has charged me to build him a house at Jerusalem, which is in Judah. (Ezra 1:2)

At the same time, the Cyrus Cylinder informs us that Cyrus gave all the credit to the Persian god Marduk.

And perhaps it might be better to ask yet another question. To what end would God employ a man like Cyrus—a brutal dictator, if truth be told? Another prophet, Jeremiah, gives us the answer:

> For I know the plans I have for you, declares the LORD, plans for welfare and not for evil, to give you a future and a hope. (Jer. 29:11)

Or as Isaiah himself wrote:

> For the sake of my servant Jacob,
>     and Israel my chosen. (Isa. 45:4)

This is God's ultimate plan—to gather His people and build His church. And in some inscrutable way, Cyrus the Persian played a role in God's plan.

> He chose us in him before the foundation of the world, that we should be holy and blameless before him. In love he predestined us for adoption as sons through Jesus Christ, according to the purpose of his will. . . . In him we have redemption through his blood, the forgiveness of our trespasses, according to the riches of his grace. . . . In him we have obtained an inheritance, having been predestined according to the purpose of him who works all things according to the counsel of his will. (Eph. 1:4–5, 7, 11)

## GOD OR GODS?

This is all very impressive, is it not? One might think that knowing God's intimate and intricate care over the future course of history might make His people more careful in acknowledging Him. Sadly, this is not the case. What we find is what we have already seen in the previous chapter: there was a burgeoning idolatry at the heart of Israel's worship. Once again, Israel needed a reminder of the *uniqueness of the one true God.*

"There's no one else!" These words might be said when suspicion has crept into a relationship. "I love you only. There's no one else that governs my heart." Yet behind such words may be a cloak of lies and deception, as well as a tearful spouse doubting the sincerity of a lover's protestations.

God's people were often unfaithful. Mimicking their neighbors, they too turned to idols—other lovers (Isa. 45:16, 20; 46:1; 48:5). In a mockingly biting refrain, God appeals to those who take refuge in man-made idols:

> To whom will you liken me and make me equal,
> > and compare me, that we may be alike?
> Those who lavish gold from the purse,
> > and weigh out silver in the scales,
> hire a goldsmith, and he makes it into a god;
> > then they fall down and worship!
> They lift it to their shoulders, they carry it,
> > they set it in its place, and it stands there;
> > it cannot move from its place.

If one cries to it, it does not answer
    or save him from his trouble. (Isa. 46:5–7)

When you cry out, let your collection of idols deliver you!
    The wind will carry them all off,
    a breath will take them away. (Isa. 57:13)

As we suggested at the end of the last chapter, we may not be impressed with the idols of the ancient Near East. They were wooden or clay statues set on shelves. Hardly impressive. But consider the idols of our own hearts. Idolatry, as David Wells puts it, is "trusting some substitute for God to serve some uniquely divine function."[9] And for us, idols take the form of the relaxation of luxury holidays, the loyalty of a sporting affiliation, or the allure of one-upmanship.

Idols cannot save, predict the future, make promises, or carry out plans. But the God who can plan and predict must be the true God, the *only* God:

I am the LORD, and there is no other,
    besides me there is no God;
    I equip you, though you do not know me,
that people may know, from the rising of the sun
    and from the west, that there is none besides me;
    I am the LORD, and there is no other. (Isa. 45:5–6)

Idolatry comes in many forms, but the most insidious are the idols we make of the things we love. Don Carson noted that when Neil Postman wrote his important book *Amusing Ourselves to Death,* he did so by contrasting two other important works: George Orwell's *1984* and Aldous Huxley's *Brave New World.* Postman concluded:

> Orwell warns that we will be overcome by an externally imposed oppression. But in Huxley's vision, no Big Brother is required to deprive people of their autonomy, maturity, and history. As he saw it, people will come to love their oppression, to adore the technologies that undo their capacities to think. . . . What Orwell feared were those who would ban books. What Huxley feared was that there would be no reason to ban a book, for there would be no one who wanted to read one. Orwell feared those who would deprive us of information. Huxley feared those who would give us so much information that we would be reduced to passivity and egoism. Orwell feared that the truth would be concealed from us. Huxley feared that the truth would be drowned in a sea of irrelevance. Orwell feared that we would become a captive culture. Huxley feared that we would become a trivial culture, preoccupied with some equivalent of the feelies, the orgy porgy, and the centrifugal bumblepuppy. In *1984,* Orwell added, people are controlled by inflicting pain. In *Brave New World* they are controlled by inflicting pleasure. In short, Orwell feared that what we hate will ruin us. Huxley feared that what we love will ruin us. This book is about the possibility that Huxley, not Orwell, was right.[10]

God is gracious. Cyrus failed to fulfill the purpose of bringing light to the nations, but God's purpose remains. God had another more glorious person and plan waiting in the shadows—Jesus. His role becomes clearer in later chapters of Isaiah's prophecy. But

Cyrus had a purpose for the immediate future: to let the Israelites return to Jerusalem and rebuild the city of God:

> He shall build my city
>     and set my exiles free. (Isa. 45:13)

To exiles in Babylon, that must have sounded like sweet music in their ears. They were not forgotten or abandoned.

# 4

# THE BURDEN-BEARING

# GOD

Listen to me, O house of Jacob,
  all the remnant of the house of Israel,
who have been borne by me from before your birth,
  carried from the womb;
even to your old age I am he,
  and to gray hairs I will carry you.
I have made, and I will bear;
  I will carry and will save. (Isa. 46:3–4)

The words of Isaiah 46:3–4 are incorporated into the familiar hymn "How Firm a Foundation":

E'en down to old age all My people shall prove
My sovereign, eternal, unchangeable love;
And when hoary hairs shall their temples adorn,
Like lambs they shall still in My bosom be borne.

This hymn was sung at the funerals of American presidents Theodore Roosevelt and Woodrow Wilson. It was also the favorite hymn of General Robert E. Lee, the Confederate general, and was sung at his funeral in the chapel of what was then called Washington College in Lexington, Va., on October 15, 1868.[1]

God cares for His people to the grave and beyond. In a prophetic picture of the future, Isaiah saw Bel (the patron god of Babylon, otherwise known as Marduk) and his son Nebo (the patron god of nearby Borsippa) unceremoniously carried away on pack animals in advance of the Persian conquest. As far as we know, it didn't occur quite like this, and Isaiah's image is just that—a metaphor describing the futility of idols, drawn from something Isaiah witnessed in his own day when Sennacherib first attacked Babylon.

And what a sight this must have been. The gods laid prostrate and wrapped in protective clothing, carried out of the city, unable to do a thing about the coming conquest. The gods were "burdens on weary beasts" (Isa. 46:1).

There is something of mockery and satire here, of course. The French sociologist Jacques Ellul wrote that humor was a peculiar way in which ancient Israel adjusted to life in foreign cultures. They "take a word and change a letter to give it a totally new sense. They play on words in such a manner as to ridicule the text or person or to achieve a very different effect."[2]

These satirical observations are more than descriptions; they are judgments. The idols of Babylon cannot save. Nebo was the god of wisdom and therefore should have foreseen the Persian advance. Every new year, he was brought to the city to "write" predictive accounts of events that were to occur in the coming year.

But Nebo failed to see the coming of Cyrus.

And as Isaiah saw the Babylonian gods weighing down the backs of poor creatures who had to carry them, the point was clear: If the gods themselves have to be carried, how can they possibly carry you?

## MOCKERY

For all of Babylon's power and pretense, her gods were worthless idols. And so God mocked Babylon. Chapter 47 of Isaiah is an example of a "taunt song" in which one nation or god taunts another in its moment of defeat. It is a song of victory. In summary:

- Babylon's luxury would be turned into the worst kind of slavery imaginable:

Your nakedness shall be uncovered,
    and your disgrace shall be seen. (Isa. 47:3)

- Babylon had employed tyranny: she showed God's people "no mercy" (Isa. 47:6).

- Pride had overtaken her. Employing claims that belong only to God, Babylon had boasted in her security and position, saying:

I am, and there is no one besides me;
I shall not sit as a widow
or know the loss of children. (Isa. 47:8)

"No one sees me," she boasted. "I am, and there is no one besides me" (Isa. 47:10).

Pride comes before a fall (Prov. 16:18), and Babylon was ripe for judgment. Her idols were powerless when the fire of God's holiness descended. Idols are always inept when it comes to facing the only true and living God.

## HOOKED ON IDOLATRY

This is not the first time we have encountered the issue of idolatry in Isaiah. It is a repeated theme because our hearts and minds are constantly replacing the one true God with false deities.

Getting what our hearts dream of could be our greatest undoing. Why? Because our hearts dream of less than they should. We were made to glorify God, but our hearts dream of self-glory. Our desires spiral into self-aggrandizing schemes of personal advancement that can never ultimately fulfill and satisfy. Nevertheless, God often grants that for which we ask. Thus, Paul warns of God's judgment: He "gave them up in the lusts of their hearts" (Rom. 1:24).

Everyone lives for something—something that captures our hearts and imaginations. These are the things we dream of because they give us hope, encouragement, and the prospect of a better tomorrow.

Adam and Eve thought it could be found in a forbidden fruit.

Abraham thought it could be found in a son for whom he had longed all his life. God put that love to the ultimate test by commanding him to sacrifice Isaac upon an altar.

Jacob wanted to be loved by his father and hoodwinked him into giving his blessing only to find his plans turn sour. As he fled from his brother's murderous threats, Jacob's life was in ruins.

Thus the biblical narrative continues, echoing the collapse of humanity into one idol after another. And before we know it, men and women are melting their jewelry and casting the molten gold into an idol. When Moses questioned his brother Aaron's role in all of this, Aaron's response seemed to echo the naïveté and seeming unconscious inevitability of idolatry: "So I said to them, 'Let any who have gold take it off.' So they gave it to me, and I threw it into the fire, and out came this calf" (Ex. 32:24).

"And out came this calf." There is a stupidity to idolatry. It is utterly unreasonable.

Isaiah provides us with a withering analysis of the utter folly of idolatry:

The ironsmith takes a cutting tool and works it over the coals. He fashions it with hammers and works it with his strong arm. He becomes hungry, and his strength fails; he drinks no water and is faint. The carpenter stretches a line; he marks it out with a pencil. He shapes it with planes and marks it with a compass. He shapes it into the figure of a man, with the beauty of a man, to dwell in a house. He cuts down cedars, or he chooses a cypress tree or an oak and lets it grow strong among the trees of the forest. He plants a cedar and the rain nourishes it. Then it becomes fuel for a man.

He takes a part of it and warms himself; he kindles a fire and bakes bread. Also he makes a god and worships it; he makes it an idol and falls down before it. Half of it he burns in the fire. Over the half he eats meat; he roasts it and is satisfied. Also he warms himself and says, "Aha, I am warm, I have seen the fire!" And the rest of it he makes into a god, his idol, and falls down to it and worships it. He prays to it and says, "Deliver me, for you are my god!"

They know not, nor do they discern, for he has shut their eyes, so that they cannot see, and their hearts, so that they cannot understand. No one considers, nor is there knowledge or discernment to say, "Half of it I burned in the fire; I also baked bread on its coals; I roasted meat and have eaten. And shall I make the rest of it an abomination? Shall I fall down before a block of wood?" He feeds on ashes; a deluded heart has led him astray, and he cannot deliver himself or say, "Is there not a lie in my right hand?" (Isa. 44:12–20)

Idols should come with a label: "Made by Man." Human ingenuity, skill, artistry, and design are the cause of their existence.

The idol is a product of someone *greater than itself.* In the process of making the idol, the one making it gets weary and exhausted. No matter how well it is made, it is still a "made thing"—inherently flawed, weak, and less than its maker.

With sharp irony, Isaiah describes how a carpenter cuts down a tree. He burns half of the wood to provide the fuel for cooking his evening supper, and the other half he makes into a god and bows down and worships it, expecting it to save him.

Dead though this idol is, it seems to grasp its maker by the hand and delude him, hiding him from reality—"the god of this world has blinded the minds of the unbelievers, to keep them from seeing" (2 Cor. 4:4).

Idolatry blinds and deafens. It is an addiction, and the addict cannot—*will* not—admit to it. "A deluded heart has led him astray, and he cannot deliver himself or say, 'Is there not a lie in my right hand?'" (Isa. 44:20).

Compulsive drug addicts or sexual offenders can hardly help themselves. They must have their fix and will do anything to have it. They are beyond reason and common sense. A powerful urge has taken hold of them. Such a thing is idolatry. It will be satisfied and will take a person captive in the process. Men and women lose their minds, and their hearts, to the idol's allurement.

When Paul visited Athens, he found a city literally filled with idols of all kinds (Acts 17:16). Idols occupied public spaces. There was Aphrodite, the goddess of beauty; Ares, the god of war; Artemis, the goddess of fertility and wealth; and Hephaestus, the god of craftsmanship. But towering over them all was the Parthenon of Athena, the goddess of wisdom, courage, inspiration, civilization, law and justice, mathematics, strength, war strategy, the arts, crafts, and skill.

Idolatry is everywhere, and we are often blind to it. Isaiah warns of the stubbornness that often grips us that makes idolatry difficult to remove. When deliverance comes, the temptation will be to give credit to the idol:

> I declared them to you from of old,
>> before they came to pass I announced them to you,

lest you should say, "My idol did them,
>    my carved image and my metal image commanded them."
(Isa. 48:5)

## IDOLS OF OUR TIME

When Cyrus came to overthrow Babylon, almost two centuries after Isaiah's vision, the Babylonian idols were powerless to stop the Persian king. Ironically, the idols were more of a burden than a help—"burdens on weary beasts" (Isa. 46:1).

Motionless and powerless, these idols could not carry the burden of the people's fear and anxiety. In need of being rescued by the gods, people found themselves instead having to rescue their gods. What good are gods like this?

As a teenager, and for reasons that now escape me, I discovered that important papers (birth certificates, insurance documents, and the like) were kept in a shoe box above a wardrobe in the downstairs bedroom that I eventually occupied. The box became something of a burden to me, especially if the house were to catch fire. I imagined that I would be held responsible for not having retrieved the precious papers. So I wrote on the side of it in large letters: "IF HOUSE ON FIRE, PLEASE GRAB!" I imagine a teenager in Babylon doing much the same thing. "If enemies are approaching, please grab Bel and Nebo!"

There is an obvious anomaly in this picture, isn't there? Gods ought not to need such rescuing. If they are capable of fulfilling our dreams and aspirations, should they not be able to deal with such potential enemies? Evidently not. When push comes to shove, they play dead.

Perhaps we do not have golden statues of deities in our homes. However, we may have man-made effigies of Jesus or Mary that function in similar ways as tokens of superstition.

And more often, our idols are subtler.

For some, it is romantic love. If only I could fall in love and find the person of my dreams, everything will be fine. Jacob was so love-struck by Rachel that he was prepared to work seven years to get her. And his shifty and duplicitous uncle Laban tricked him into marrying her less pretty older sister, granting him Rachel also on condition that Jacob work for him another seven years. Jacob worshiped the ground Rachel trod on, and he was prepared to do anything—*anything*—to have her. And what it reaped was disaster. He favored Rachel over Leah, and his home became a nightmare.

When an older man leaves his wife for a younger woman, it is an addiction to a promise that cannot deliver. It leaves in its wake ruination and despair. Serving the idol of (what we think of as) love can cost us a marriage, a friendship, and a peaceful conscience.

## SUCCESS

For others, Bel and Nebo take the form of success in business and career. Timothy Keller, in his insightful book on idolatry, makes the point crystal clear:

> More than other idols, personal success and achievement lead to a sense that we ourselves are god, that our security and value rest in

our own wisdom, strength, and performance. To be the very best at what you do, to be at the top of the heap, means no one else is like you. You are supreme.[3]

Success, we come to think, will keep us safe when trouble comes. It may even keep us from trouble. And then disease strikes and all the success in the world is incapable of fighting the illness. Success merely gave us hope for this world, but none for the world to come. Death is the great leveler, and as the raided tombs of the pharaohs tell us, we cannot take our earthly success into the world to come.

The Heidelberg Catechism begins with a well-known question: "What is your only comfort in life and in death?" In its answer lies the cure for idolatry:

That I am not my own, but belong—body and soul, in life and in death—to my faithful Savior, Jesus Christ. He has fully paid for all my sins with his precious blood, and has set me free from the tyranny of the devil. He also watches over me in such a way that not a hair can fall from my head without the will of my Father in heaven; in fact, all things must work together for my salvation. Because I belong to him, Christ, by his Holy Spirit, assures me of eternal life and makes me wholeheartedly willing and ready from now on to live for him.

## BURDENS ARE LIFTED AT CALVARY

Other idols are far subtler than money, sex, and power. They are convictions that promise meaning and value without reference to God. Sports, recreation, the weekend, education, a particular office or position in society or church, politics, America. The list is endless, since anything that takes the place of God is an idol.

Yet these convictions consistently fail. They cannot carry us through the trials of life. Only God can do that.

In the space of two verses, Isaiah provides a fourfold allusion to God as a burden carrier:

> Listen to me, O house of Jacob,
>> all the remnant of the house of Israel,
> who have been *borne* by me from before your birth,
>> *carried* from the womb;
> even to your old age I am he,
>> and to gray hairs I will *carry* you.
> I have made, and I will bear;
>> I will *carry* and will save." (Isa. 46:3–4, emphasis added)

Different words are employed here that are translated "carried" or "carry." The verbs are echoed later in the fourth Servant Song as a depiction of what Messiah would do when He came to redeem His people. It is not Cyrus who would carry God's people, but the Suffering Servant:

> Surely he has *borne* our griefs
> and *carried* our sorrows. . . . (Isa. 53:4, emphasis added)

> . . . and he shall *bear* [carry] their iniquities. (Isa. 53:11, emphasis added)

It is Jesus, finally, who carries our burdens. He carried our sins to the cross. And weighed down by the burden of these sins, He lost sight of His father's love and embrace: "My God, my God, why have you forsaken me?" (Matt. 27:46). As our substitute and sin bearer, He took the wrath that our sins deserved and bore it to the full. He is our deliverer, burden carrier, and propitiator.

And because, through faith, we are now Jesus' brothers and sisters, He continues to carry our sorrows.

> From sinking sand He lifted me,
> with tender hand He lifted me,
> from shades of night to plains of light,
> O praise His name, He lifted me![4]

## E'EN DOWN TO OLD AGE

The breadth of God's commitment to carry us is astounding:

> Listen to me, O house of Jacob,
>    all the remnant of the house of Israel,
> who have been borne by me from before your birth,
>    carried from the womb;
> even to your old age I am he,
>    and to gray hairs I will carry you.
> I have made, and I will bear;
>    I will carry and will save. (Isa. 46:3–4)

Note the sweep of life: "before your birth . . . from the womb [growing through childhood and adolescence] . . . old age . . . gray hairs." In every stage of life from the womb to the tomb, God cares and carries.

Growing old is difficult. It is a humbling and sometimes humiliating experience. It is the experience of "ageism"—when younger generations speak patronizingly of you because of your gray hairs (or lack of hair!). Passed over for promotion because the firm is looking for "younger guys." The mandated retirement policy and the enforced exchange of life in the fast lane for life in the slow lane. Growing old is not for wimps.[5]

Yet God promises to carry our burdens and make them His burdens, even the burden of growing old.

He will never leave us or forsake His own (Deut. 31:6; Heb. 13:5).

EPILOGUE

Earlier in this chapter, we noted that Babylon fell under the weight of her own internal pressure to give credit to worthless idols. But exactly who or what is *Babylon*? "Babylon" refers not only to the dominant world empire of the sixth century but also to the archetypal human rebellion of Babel—a culture of human autonomy and rebellion against God (see Gen. 11).

Babylon occurs again in the biblical narrative in Revelation. The last book of the Bible describes the destruction of Babylon along with her servants, the Beast of the Sea and the earth, typically interpreted as the forces of religious and secular defiance against God:

Fallen, fallen is Babylon the great!
>   She has become a dwelling place for demons,
a haunt for every unclean spirit,
>   a haunt for every unclean bird,
>   a haunt for every unclean and detestable beast.
For all nations have drunk
>   the wine of the passion of her sexual immorality,
and the kings of the earth have committed immorality with her,
>   and the merchants of the earth have grown rich from the power
>   of her luxurious living. (Rev. 18:2–3)

Babylon and all her idols will fall. Her idols are worthless. They cannot carry your burdens.

Only Jesus can do that.

And He will. Just ask Him.

"Listen" the prophet says, and "remember" (Isa. 46:3, 12; 46:8–9).

# THE SERVANT,

# JESUS

Behold my servant, whom I uphold,
    my chosen, in whom my soul delights. (Isa. 42:1)

For he grew up before him like a young plant,
    and like a root out of dry ground;
he had no form or majesty that we should look at him,
    and no beauty that we should desire him.
He was despised and rejected by men,
    a man of sorrows and acquainted with grief;
and as one from whom men hide their faces
    he was despised, and we esteemed him not. (Isa. 53:2–3)

"There is no peace . . . for the wicked" (Isa. 48:22).

These startling words are not addressed to the heathen nations but to God's covenant people. They describe the people's condition after their return to the Promised Land from exile. They are a lament. The people have learned so little in their captivity.

The reason for their exile is spelled out with a solemn indictment: they had sinned against the Lord, "in whose ways they would not walk, and whose law they would not obey" (Isa. 42:24).

They returned to Jerusalem the way they had left it.

What Israel needed was salvation.

What Israel needed was a Savior. One who would come from "outside of themselves."[1] What Israel (Judah) needed was a Servant-Savior who would do what she evidently could not do for herself.

This also is our need.

And God had good news for His rebellious people, news built upon His "covenant love" (*hesed*) for them (Isa. 54:8, 10).[2]


## PROMISES, PROMISES

The prophecy of Isaiah made promises that were difficult to fulfill.

Chapters 2 and 11 depict a united, transformed world, but there is no sign of that when the exiled Hebrews return to the ruins of Jerusalem.[3]

Chapter 9 suggests a glorious David-like kingdom, but there is no sign of this reality on the horizon.[4]

Are these promises more like aspirations than certainties? Longings of what might have been rather than what actually did occur?

No, there is more than wishful thinking here. These promises find partial fulfillment in the dawning of the new covenant era: the incarnation, life, death, and resurrection of Jesus; the significance of Pentecost; and the spread of the church from Jerusalem to "the end of the earth" (Acts 1:8).

And to bring this larger canvas into reality, a Messiah-figure is promised. His depiction is threefold:

1. A *King*, like David, who will rule and reign over an expansive, worldwide kingdom (see Isa. 1:26–27; 7:14; 9:7; 11:1; 32:1–6; 33:17–24).

2. A *Servant*, depicted in four "songs" (Isa. 42:1–4; 49:1–6; 50:4–9; 52:13–53:12). Twice, the servant is identified as Israel,[5] but it is immediately apparent that she cannot be the sinless servant depicted in these songs. She has neither character nor desire to fulfill this role. On the other hand, the true servant is a revealer of truth,[6] perfect, obedient, and explicitly, a substitutionary sin bearer who voluntarily dies and lives again to clothe His people with His own righteousness.

3. An *anointed Conqueror*. As Isaiah looks forward, he anticipates one who is anointed by the Spirit, engaging in both salvation and vengeance, blessing and cursing (see Isa. 59:21; 61:1–3; 61:10–62:7; 63:1–7).

And it becomes increasingly clear that the Messiah will come for both the covenant community and the gentiles (the nations):

> I will give you as a covenant for the people,
>     a light for the nations. (Isa. 42:6)

We might have expected that this responsibility would have been fulfilled by the covenant people themselves. Had they not been told that their joyful obedience would lead the nations to say, "Surely this great nation is a wise and understanding people" (Deut. 4:6)? But, as we have seen, God's people in Isaiah's day are "blind" and "deaf" (Isa. 42:18–19; 43:8).

If not Israel, then who?

And the answer is another King-Servant-anointed Conqueror—Jesus.

From the corridors of the eighth century BC, Isaiah saw the coming of Jesus who would bring redemption and restoration.

This is why Isaiah is called "the evangelical prophet"—his entire focus is on the *evangel*, the "good news" of the gospel.

Good news for sinners like you and me.

# 5

# THE WATERS

# OF LIFE

Come, everyone who thirsts,
    come to the waters;
and he who has no money,
    come, buy and eat!
Come, buy wine and milk
    without money and without price. (Isa. 55:1)

Shame—it cripples and shrinks us. It drains motivation and energy. Carl Jung, the Swiss psychiatrist and founder of analytical psychology, was correct when he wrote, "Shame is a soul eating emotion."[1]

To be more accurate, there is good and bad shame. The Apostle Paul, for example, tells the Corinthians, "Wake up from your drunken stupor, as is right, and do not go on sinning. For some have no knowledge of God. I say this to your shame"

(1 Cor. 15:34). The shame referenced here is well placed. They ought to feel shame. Shame of this kind can lead to repentance.

But what if the shame lingers too long? In that case, it can demonstrate a distrust in the promises of God and a loss of confidence in the gospel. Or what if we feel shame for something we didn't do? The shame felt in these circumstances may seriously hinder and debilitate our Christian walk. It is to this that Isaiah now turns, promising in chapter 54 a time when Israel will "forget her shame" (v. 4). Can such a thing be possible?

Chapters 54 and 55 of Isaiah belong together. They form the twin themes of the prophet's message.[2]

Chapter 54 is concerned with Judah—that is, God's covenant people.

Chapter 55 takes up the theme of the implications of the Servant's work upon the nations of the world.

Chapter 54 views the expansion of the kingdom by employing the symbolism of the city of Zion. The city will grow and expand in a manner that defies explanation or anticipation.

We are familiar with the concept of city expansion. Think of cities like Hangzhou, Tianjin, Shanghai, Nanjing, Chengdu, Hyderabad, Ahmedabad, Riyadh, Karachi. These are among the world's fastest growing cities. The populations of these cities are expanding at alarming rates as urbanization occurs around the world.

Multiplying metaphors, Isaiah combines concepts involving shame or disgrace—a widow unable to support herself (Isa. 54:4) and a deserted wife (Isa. 54:6)—suggesting that a time will come when the shame associated with unfulfilled expectations will disappear. Zion, a barren woman, will suddenly need to expand her property to accommodate her growing family, as they in turn populate the otherwise desolate cities:

> Enlarge the place of your tent,
>> and let the curtains of your habitations be stretched out;
> do not hold back; lengthen your cords
>> and strengthen your stakes.
> For you will spread abroad to the right and to the left,
>> and your offspring will possess the nations
>> and will people the desolate cities. (Isa. 54:2–3)

And shame and guilt will be no more.

> Fear not, for you will not be ashamed;
>> be not confounded, for you will not be disgraced;
> for you will forget the shame of your youth,
>> and the reproach of your widowhood you will remember no more. (Isa. 54:4)

The Servant's work ensures the eradication of shame and guilt. There will be "no memory" of sin.

The shame was God's chastisement. It was "for a moment" (Isa. 54:8), and His chastisements hurt. But He will not abandon His people or break His covenant. As He gave to Noah the rainbow as a sign and seal of His covenant of preservation (Isa. 54:9), so our God promises never to abandon His covenant love.

> "For the mountains may depart
>> and the hills be removed,

but my steadfast love shall not depart from you,
    and my covenant of peace shall not be removed,"
    says the Lord, who has compassion on you. (Isa. 54:10)

The Servant has borne the chastisement that brought us peace:

But he was pierced for our transgressions;
    he was crushed for our iniquities;
upon him was the chastisement that brought us peace,
    and with his wounds we are healed. (Isa. 53:5)

And in the place of barrenness and desolation come life and progeny—in abundance.

The prophet describes a beautiful city, the building blocks of the description of the new Jerusalem in Revelation 21.

O afflicted one, storm-tossed and not comforted,
    behold, I will set your stones in antimony,
    and lay your foundations with sapphires.
I will make your pinnacles of agate,
    your gates of carbuncles,
    and all your wall of precious stones.
All your children shall be taught by the Lord,
    and great shall be the peace of your children.
In righteousness you shall be established;
    you shall be far from oppression, for you shall not fear;
    and from terror, for it shall not come near you.
If anyone stirs up strife,
    it is not from me;

whoever stirs up strife with you
    shall fall because of you.
Behold, I have created the smith
    who blows the fire of coals
    and produces a weapon for its purpose.
I have also created the ravager to destroy;
    no weapon that is fashioned against you shall succeed,
    and you shall refute every tongue that rises against you in
    judgment.
This is the heritage of the servants of the LORD
    and their vindication from me, declares the LORD.
    (Isa. 54:11–17)

This city is secure and protected, filled with sons and daughters who are Yahweh's disciples (Isa. 54:13).[3]

A dream? Only to those who are asleep to God's promises.

## GOD'S COVENANT

From the populated, secure city filled with the sound of those praising the Lord, the focus shifts from Israel to the "peoples"[4] or "nation."[5] The main thought centers on the idea of a covenant—a relationship with God and all that this entails.

From the very beginning, God intended the world to be blessed. This was made clear in the initial pronouncement of the covenant to Abraham: "in you all the families of the earth shall be blessed" (Gen. 12:3).

In Isaiah 55, it is David, not Abraham, who is in view. Citing Psalm 89, Isaiah reminds his readers of these wonderful words:

I will make with you an everlasting covenant,
my steadfast, sure love for David. (Isa. 55:3)

Unusually, a plural form of God's covenant love is employed (and translated above as "steadfast, sure love") (Ps. 89:1, 49).[6] God's covenant love is doubly sure, doubly trustworthy.

Psalm 89 is deeply significant for one special reason: it is a testimony to God's covenantal faithfulness *to David*. In the original account of the covenant in 2 Samuel 7, the word "covenant" does not appear. It is here, in Psalm 89, that justification is forthcoming for understanding the account as a covenant inauguration ceremony.

At the close of 2 Samuel, David reflects on the deep significance of God's faithfulness:

The Spirit of the LORD speaks by me;
his word is on my tongue.
The God of Israel has spoken;
the Rock of Israel has said to me:
When one rules justly over men,
ruling in the fear of God,
he dawns on them like the morning light,
like the sun shining forth on a cloudless morning,
like rain that makes grass to sprout from the earth.
For does not my house stand so with God?
For he has made with me an everlasting covenant,
ordered in all things and secure. (2 Sam. 23:2–5b)

Just think for a minute about David's life—the failures that occupied so much of it. How then could he possibly find confidence that God would not forsake him? The answer is a one-word, theologically packed term—covenant (Hebrew *berith*). God's covenant is "ordered" and "everlasting." It is a theme the psalmist returns to in Psalm 89, the words cited in Isaiah 55:3:

> I will sing of the steadfast love [lit. *loves*] of the LORD, forever;
>> with my mouth I will make known your faithfulness to all
>> generations.
> For I said, "Steadfast love will be built up forever;
>> in the heavens you will establish your faithfulness."
> You have said, "I have made a covenant with my chosen one;
>> I have sworn to David my servant:
> 'I will establish your offspring forever,
>> and build your throne for all generations.'" (Ps. 89:1–4)

As the psalm unfolds, two ideas emerge that explain the plural "loves" of the psalm's opening and closing.

1. "My faithfulness and my steadfast love shall be with him": ensuring that his enemies will not outwit him, and that his foes will be struck down (Ps. 89:22–24).

2. "My steadfast love I will keep for him forever, and my covenant will stand firm for him": ensuring that David's offspring will endure forever and his throne will last forever—as long as the sun and moon endure (Ps. 89:28, 36–37).

A worldwide, cosmic Davidic kingdom that in some sense will last forever. How can this be? Perhaps we need some clues:

- The gospel of Matthew gives the genealogical proof that Jesus, in His humanity, is a direct descendant of Abraham and David through Joseph, Jesus' legal father. The genealogy in Luke 3 traces Jesus' lineage through His mother, Mary. Jesus is a descendant of David by adoption through Joseph and by blood through Mary.
- Paul's letter to the Romans begins with the assertion that Jesus was "descended from David according to the flesh" (Matt. 1:1–6; Luke 3:23–38; Rom. 1:3).
- And the book of Acts ends with this confident note: "Therefore let it be known to you that this salvation of God has been sent to the Gentiles; they will listen" (Acts 28:28).

What David and Isaiah glimpse from afar is the spread of the gospel to the nations of the world, something we have witnessed in our time. It is an unfinished expansion, of course. But it *is* happening.

Too often, those of us who live in the United States or in Europe view things from a warped perspective. But, as Mark Noll has so helpfully said:

- "Active Christian adherence has become more active in Africa than in Europe."
- "The number of practicing Christians in China may be approaching the number in the United Sates."
- "Live bodies in church are far more numerous in Kenya than in Canada."

- "More believers worship together in church Sunday by Sunday in Nagaland than in Norway."
- "More Christian workers from Brazil are active in cross-cultural ministry outside their homeland than from Britain or from Canada."
- "Last Sunday . . . more believers attended church in China than in all of so-called 'Christian Europe.'"
- "This past Sunday more Anglicans attended church in each of Kenya, South Africa, Tanzania, and Uganda, than did Anglicans in Britain and Canada and Episcopalians in the United States combined."
- "Last Sunday more Presbyterians were in church in Ghana than in Scotland."[7]

Seen from this perspective, Isaiah's prophecy is being fulfilled.


## COVENANT MERCY

Confidence in God's work in *our* lives springs from this same covenant: "I will make with you an everlasting covenant" (Isa. 55:3).

If there is one word that summarizes everything that God designs for the universe, it is *covenant*.

If there is one word that summarizes God's redemptive design for sinners—assuring them of forgiveness and restoration—it is *covenant*.

But what exactly is a covenant? Perhaps a better question would be, what exactly is a *biblical* covenant? A covenant is a binding, solemn agreement with accompanying promises and threats. In the Bible, God is the One who initiates and designs the terms of the covenant. Biblical covenants involving God are never the result of a bartering session with compromises reflecting differing viewpoints. Covenants in the Bible reflect God's initiative, sovereignty, passion, and enduring care.

There is a basic grammar to biblical covenants. God binds Himself to His people, and they in turn commit themselves to follow Him. It is never the other way around.

Covenant spells G-R-A-C-E.

As Sinclair Ferguson puts it, "The pattern is, 'I will, therefore you should'; not 'I will, but only if you will first.'"[8]

The pattern of biblical covenants provides for us a key, a hermeneutic (principle of interpretation) that provides a way of understanding the Bible as a whole. Indeed, the entire message of redemption may be viewed as an unfolding series of successive covenants (with Adam, Noah, Abraham, Moses, and David, and a promise of a new covenant). Viewed as a whole, we sometimes speak of them as one covenant—the covenant of grace. While there are nuanced differences that apply to particular epochs of redemptive history, there is also a core that remains essentially the same throughout: God's gospel initiative to redeem His people and provide for them a place to live out their lives for eternity.

One covenant. One administration of grace.

Viewing successive biblical covenants this way helps us see a line of continuity from the Old Testament (the old covenant) to the New Testament (the new covenant). The same Lord is doing essentially the *same* thing in both testaments, one in the shadow and the other in the light.

Returning to Isaiah, covenant life is like a banquet, with food and drink in abundance: "eat," "milk," "wine," "bread," "rich food" (Isa. 55:1–2). And at the close of chapter 55, there are more allusions to "joy," "peace," and "singing" (Isa. 55:12).

## A NEW ORDER OF BEING

Isaiah employs rich metaphors:

> Instead of the thorn shall come up the cypress;
>> instead of the brier shall come up the myrtle. (Isa. 55:13)

"Cypress" and "myrtle" signify that a forest-garden will grow in rich display of abundance and fruitfulness—the curse replaced by the blessing. A transformed people in a transformed world.

We will return to this later, at the close this book, but a few thoughts here will serve as an anticipation. Isaiah views a new world order, involving first of all a new relationship to the world we now live in, which will allow us to see it differently, in a manner we have not done before. But this new world order ultimately refers to "a new heavens and a new earth" (Isa. 65:17–25; 66:22).

The "thorn" and "briar" that are so much a part of our current existence are aspects of what Paul calls "futility."[9] Our current creation life is under a curse. But Isaiah anticipates a new world order, without the futility that mars this current world.

And it will be like an "everlasting sign" (Isa. 55:13) of God's gracious mercy and foreordained plan. This is what the Anointed King-Servant will accomplish.

## THE INVITATION

Come, everyone who thirsts,
    come to the waters;
and he who has no money,
    come, buy and eat!
Come, buy wine and milk
    without money and without price.
Why do you spend your money for that which is not bread,
    and your labor for that which does not satisfy?
Listen diligently to me, and eat what is good,
    and delight yourselves in rich food.
Incline your ear, and come to me;
    hear, that your soul may live. (Isa. 55:1–3)

Come, incline your ear and listen, buy and eat, seek, return to the Lord. These are the urgent exhortations.

To whom are these invitations made? Two kinds of people are in view.

First, the offer is made to those who are thirsty and hungry. The destitute. Those who have come to the end of themselves. The ones whose expectations and hopes have shriveled and died. Optimism has vanquished.

Andrew Delbanco's cultural analysis of modern America proposes a fascinating thesis. Human beings cannot, he suggests, simply live in the present. They have to discern connections, both to the past and more especially, to the future. There has to be some way in which we feel ourselves part of a story that leads somewhere. Without it, optimism dies. "We must imagine some end to life that transcends our own tiny allotment of days and hours," Delbanco writes, "if we are to keep at bay the dim back-of-the-mind suspicion that we are adrift in an absurd world."[10]

Isaiah offers confidence for those who have lost all sense of hope. He offers meaning and purpose where there is only vanity and despair. When all you have is an ache or a longing, there is an invitation to salvation and wholeness.

The second offer is made to a different category of people. If the first group had no money, the second is spending it as though it were going out of fashion.

Why do you spend your money for that which is not bread,
    and your labor for that which does not satisfy? (Isa. 55:2)

The disappointment of success! You earn money only to put it into "a bag with holes" (Hag. 1:6).

Consider the problem addressed by the Preacher in Ecclesiastes:

I made great works. I built houses and planted vineyards for myself. . . . I also gathered for myself silver and gold and the treasure of kings and provinces. I got singers, both men and women, and many concubines, the delight of the sons of man. . . . And whatever my eyes desired I did not keep from them. I kept my heart from no pleasure, for my heart found pleasure. (Eccl. 2:4, 8, 10)

Nothing brought him happiness. Satisfaction eluded him. "I hated life," he concludes (Eccl. 2:17).

Most of us are in denial about the levels of our satisfaction with life. When asked, "How are you?" we instinctively reply, "Fine!" "I'm OK." Who, after all, wants to hear an honest answer to this question?

"Actually, do you have a few hours while I tell you how depressing and disappointing my life is just now?"

For some of us, there is a nagging sense that something is missing, even if we can't quite put our finger on what that is. Assuming that satisfaction is possible, we join the rest of our secular world by riding the treadmill of acquisition: jobs, stuff, sex, and so on. And as long as we think that eventually, with better jobs, stuff, and sex, that satisfaction will be realized, we are far too busy to notice how discontented we actually are. We are still chasing the dream.

For others, there is a nagging suspicion that "a dream" is all it is. "It"—whatever "it" is—has no reality. "It" cannot be found. Therefore, they step off the treadmill, succumbing to a cynicism about the possibility of satisfaction. "Life is tough and then you die!" "I am just trying to live the best I can."

To both the hopeless and the dissatisfied, Isaiah offers confidence and fulfillment.

## HEALING

In the gospel of John, Jesus addresses a crowd about the "bread of life." Whoever eats this bread "shall not hunger" (John 6:35). Like Isaiah, Jesus warns about the fruitless possibility of seeking for satisfaction in the wrong places. He warns about "food that perishes" (John 6:27).

And Jesus' remedy is not simply to say, "I will give you the bread that satisfies." Rather, what He says is this: "I am the bread of life; whoever comes to me shall not hunger" (John 6:35). The solution to the problem of sin and misery is believing in Jesus Christ as our Lord and Savior.

Jesus offers bread to him who has "no money." He offers life-giving, life-sustaining nourishment "without money and without price" (Isa. 55:1). How can this be? The answer lies in the fourth Servant Song: Jesus paid it all Himself.

> But he was pierced for our transgressions;
>> he was crushed for our iniquities;
> upon him was the chastisement that brought us peace,
>> and with his wounds we are healed.
> All we like sheep have gone astray;
>> we have turned—every one—to his own way;
> and the LORD has laid on him
>> the iniquity of us all. (Isa. 53:5–6)

If you are far away from God, you need to come back to the Savior.

If you have drawn near, but only to gaze from a discreet distance, you need to come and eat and drink at the Master's feet.

If you have taken the bread and the cup He offers, but have simply held it in your hands, you need to eat the bread and drink from the cup. It is not enough simply to study it.

## FAITH AND REPENTANCE

Seek . . . call . . . forsake . . . return (Isa. 55:6–7).

These four exhortations collectively summarize the need for both faith *and* repentance. The Puritan preacher and writer Thomas Watson wrote: "The two great graces essential to a saint in this life, are faith and repentance. These are the two wings by which he flies to heaven."[11]

Calling 911 isn't that difficult. Even children have been known to do it when they discover a sick parent.

"Lord, I need you" is all we need to say, and the response will be immediate. It requires no advanced degrees in metaphysics or philosophy.

*But I hardly know God exists!* That may be true, but you will get to know Him better if you come to Him.

"While he is near. . . ." In a sense, He is never far away. He is everywhere at all times. But we are not always ready to acknowledge that. And, though we may find this difficult to accept, God may withdraw for a season and leave our hearts to their own desires and inclinations. If we are honest, our hearts have not always desired Him.

This is especially true if we desire our sins more than the thought of fellowship with God. Yet repentance is essential if our relationship with God is going to be genuine. There is a cultural narrative that suggests that God loves us "just the way we are." But this is unsubtle. God loves us, but it cost Him His Son's life. He has only ever loved One "the way he is"—His sinless Son. He loves *in Christ*. We come to Him, and call upon Him, "just as we are." But we cannot remain "just as we are."

> Let the wicked forsake his way,
>> and the unrighteous man his thoughts. (Isa. 55:7)

Forsake *and* turn. Paul referred to the "turning" that true repentance involves when he wrote of the Thessalonian Christians, noting how they had "turned to God from idols to serve the living and true God" (1 Thess. 1:9).

But how is any of this possible? Can I really find salvation? Can my sins—*my* sins—be forgiven? I feel utterly unable to do this.

In ourselves, we cannot do any of what is asked of us in this passage. We need the power of the Word of God.

> For my thoughts are not your thoughts,
>> neither are your ways my ways, declares the LORD.
> For as the heavens are higher than the earth,
>> so are my ways higher than your ways
>> and my thoughts than your thoughts.
>
> For as the rain and the snow come down from heaven
>> and do not return there but water the earth,
> making it bring forth and sprout,
>> giving seed to the sower and bread to the eater,
> so shall my word be that goes out from my mouth;
>> it shall not return to me empty,
> but it shall accomplish that which I purpose,
>> and shall succeed in the thing for which I sent it. (Isa. 55:8–11)

Note what is said here about God's Word:

- God's Word is superior. There is an infinite chasm separating us from God. His ways and thoughts are not our ways and thoughts. God's assessment of our need and our own assessment are very different. The problem we have is simply that we fail to grasp what our need is.
- God's Word is powerful. Like rain that causes otherwise dead seed to come to life and grow and be fruitful, God's Word—the Scriptures—brings otherwise dead sinners to life and fruitfulness. It is a life-giving, life-enriching Word.
- God's Word is effective. The Word of God perfectly and completely accomplishes God's purpose. The salvation of the lost, the calling of the gentiles, the building of Christ's church, the restoration of Eden—all these will be achieved just as God has promised by the power of the Word of God.

Just the Bible, expounded, heralded, and believed.

For the word of God is living and active, sharper than any two-edged sword, piercing to the division of soul and of spirit, of joints and of marrow, and discerning the thoughts and intentions of the heart. (Heb. 4:12)

I heard the voice of Jesus say,
"Come unto Me and rest;
Lay down, thou weary one, lay down,
Thy head upon My breast."

I came to Jesus as I was,
Weary and worn and sad;
I found in Him a resting-place,
And He has made me glad.

I heard the voice of Jesus say,
"Behold, I freely give
The living water; thirsty one,
Stoop down and drink and live."
I came to Jesus, and I drank
Of that life-giving stream.
My thirst was quenched, my soul revived,
And now I live in Him.[12]

# 6

# A WELL-WATERED

# GARDEN

Is not this the fast that I choose:
  to loose the bonds of wickedness,
  to undo the straps of the yoke,
to let the oppressed go free,
  and to break every yoke?
Is it not to share your bread with the hungry
  and bring the homeless poor into your house;
when you see the naked, to cover him,
  and not to hide yourself from your own flesh?
Then shall your light break forth like the dawn,
  and your healing shall spring up speedily;
your righteousness shall go before you;
  the glory of the LORD shall be your rear guard.
Then you shall call, and the LORD will answer;
  you shall cry, and he will say, "Here I am." (Isa. 58:6–9)

We are saved by grace alone, through faith alone, *apart* from the works of the law.[1] But the faith we express is never alone, it is always *accompanied* by works. The Westminster Confession of Faith puts it this way:

> Faith, thus receiving and resting on Christ and His righteousness, is the alone instrument of justification: yet is it not alone in the person justified, but is ever accompanied with all other saving graces, and is no dead faith, but works by love.[2]

Faith is a busy little thing. Luther wrote:

> Oh, it is a living, busy, active, mighty thing, this faith. And so it is impossible for it not to do good works incessantly. It does not ask whether there are good works to do, but before the question rises, it has already done them, and is always at the doing of them.[3]

We are saved in order to do the very works that God intends us to do. "For we are his workmanship, created in Christ Jesus for good works, which God prepared beforehand, that we should walk in them" (Eph. 2:10). Elsewhere, we are urged to be "zealous for good works" (Titus 2:14). And Jesus urged in the Sermon on the Mount, "let your light shine before others, so that they may see your good works and give glory to your Father who is in heaven" (Matt. 5:16).

Isaiah 58 is an urgent call to action, to *doing*. Specifically, as we shall see, this entails acts of mercy and justice.

And the promise given is that if we do this, we will experience a delight in God:

You shall take delight in the LORD,
and I will make you ride on the heights of the earth. (Isa. 58:14)

A *joy*ride—the ride of your life.

What could possibly bring about such an experience? The answer is unexpected and surprising—the Sabbath.

Really? So many Christians have such a low view of the Sabbath that Isaiah's words sound puzzling indeed. Can the Sabbath produce genuine joy and gladness? And do Isaiah's words having anything to say to us today? Before we answer these questions, we need to explore a little deeper the way the prophet arrives at this conclusion.

## TRUE AND FALSE RELIGION

Chapters 58 and 59 of Isaiah describe two very contrasting worlds. One (chapter 59) is reality; the other (chapter 58) is an ideal world. The reality is that God's people are failures and compromisers. When Paul in Romans 3 cites a number of Old Testament passages to underline humanity's sinfulness—and therefore its need for the gospel—one of the citations comes from Isaiah 59:

Their feet run to evil,
and they are swift to shed innocent blood;
their thoughts are thoughts of iniquity;
desolation and destruction are in their highways.
The way of peace they do not know. (Isa. 59:7–8)[4]

Sin abounds. It is the "transgression" and "sins" that form the opening thought of Isaiah 58:

Cry aloud; do not hold back;
>lift up your voice like a trumpet;
declare to my people their transgression,
>to the house of Jacob their sins. (Isa. 58:1)

And where does sin manifest itself most clearly? In our *religion*. Counterintuitive as this may sound, our greatest crimes lie in our piety.

But wait. Doesn't the prophet describe works of piety like fasting and praying? Indeed, he does.

Yet they seek me daily
>and delight to know my ways,
as if they were a nation that did righteousness
>and did not forsake the judgment of their God;
they ask of me righteous judgments;
>they delight to draw near to God. (Isa. 58:2)

Is the Lord not pleased with all this religious fervor? Apparently not. So what could possibly be wrong with it?

In Isaiah's time, men and women prayed and fasted, and then went about doing their own business according to their own agendas. They said one thing in worship and did another in practice.

Behold, in the day of your fast you seek your own pleasure,
>and oppress all your workers.

Behold, you fast only to quarrel and to fight
　　and to hit with a wicked fist. (Isa. 58:3–4)


## SOCIAL JUSTICE AND REAL-WORLD MERCY

Will Sunday worship produce Monday mercy and Friday fairness? That is the issue before us in this section of Isaiah.

Piety devoid of consequent acts of mercy is empty and meaningless. And God says plainly:

Fasting like yours this day
　　will not make your voice to be heard on high. (Isa. 58:4)


What exactly does God require? What does social justice and practical mercy look like? Again, the prophet spells it out:

Is not this the fast that I choose:
　　to loose the bonds of wickedness,
　　to undo the straps of the yoke,
to let the oppressed go free,
　　and to break every yoke?
Is it not to share your bread with the hungry
　　and bring the homeless poor into your house;
when you see the naked, to cover him,
　　and not to hide yourself from your own flesh? . . .
If you take away the yoke from your midst,
　　the pointing of the finger, and speaking wickedness. . . .
　　(Isa. 58:6–7, 9)

Five principal features emerge as matters of concern:

- Exploitation
- Hunger
- Housing/shelter
- Clothing
- Verbal abuse and false accusation

It's quite a list: concern for workers' rights; a desire for social justice; a willingness to help the poor and indigent, the homeless; the use of abusive language.

Frankly, some of us wish these things would go away and leave us alone. We want to curl up with a nice book by a warm fire and have a quiet time with Jesus. But if that is all we do, if that's all there is to our profession of faith, then our faith is empty. Our testimony to Jesus is a sham.

Of course, Isaiah is concerned about the purity of the gospel, too. It is vital that the message of salvation be proclaimed clearly and without compromise. But it is also vital that the evidence of the gospel be visible in our lives—that we become Jesus-like. And the shape of Jesus-likeness is identified with a passionate concern for human need.

In a recent blog post after a presidential election, Jonathan Leeman wrote:

> Paul asked the Jews of his day, "You who preach against stealing, do you steal?"
>
> I've got a few questions of my own. You who call for immigration reform, do you practice hospitality with strangers?

You who vote for family values, do you honor your parents and love your spouse sacrificially?

You who speak against abortion, do you physically and emotionally defraud your girlfriend? Let worldly ambition delay having children? Never make it home in time for the soccer game? Quietly acquiesce to abortion when push comes to shove? Do you embrace and assist the single mothers in your church? Do you encourage adoption?

You who talk about welfare reform, do you give to the needy in your congregation?

You who proclaim that all lives matter, who are your friends? Do they all look like you?

You who rightly lament structural injustices, do you work against them in your own congregation? Do you rejoice with those who rejoice, and weep with those who weep?

You who fight for traditional marriage, do you submit to your husband, or love your wife, cherishing her as you would your own body and washing her with the water of the Word?

You who are concerned about the economy and the job market, do you obey your boss with a sincere heart, not as a people-pleaser but as you would obey Christ?

You who care about corporate tax rates, how do you treat your employees? Do you threaten them, forgetting that he who is both their Master and yours is in heaven, and that there is no partiality with him?[5]

This is very convicting, indeed. Most of us are rendered guilty by these measurements.

But there are blessings that come to us when we do what God desires of us. This is not a crass health-and-wealth point of view. Rather, it is the perspective of the Beatitudes: there is "blessedness" that attends the meek, the poor in spirit, the peacemakers (Matt. 5:3–12). When you live out the life of the Spirit, you discover who and what you are.

We need to examine chapter 58 a little more carefully.

## THE SABBATH

Looking at Isaiah 58 as a whole brings out a fascinating structural element. Isaiah 58 begins with a *fast without a blessing* and ends with a *feast with a blessing*.[6]

It is one thing to impose laws and ceremonies that God has not commanded and make this everything. It is another to neglect laws and ceremonies that God has commanded and think this is nothing.

> If you turn back your foot from the Sabbath,
>> from doing your pleasure on my holy day,
> and call the Sabbath a delight
>> and the holy day of the LORD honorable;
> if you honor it, not going your own ways,
>> or seeking your own pleasure, or talking idly;
> then you shall take delight in the LORD,
>> and I will make you ride on the heights of the earth;
> I will feed you with the heritage of Jacob your father,
>> for the mouth of the LORD has spoken. (Isa. 58:13–14)[7]

Talk of the Sabbath puts most Christians on the defensive. A typical response might be: "You surely don't think we shouldn't allow the children to play in the garden on Sundays, do you?"

Questions of specious reasoning (casuistry) arise quick-ly—"Can I do *x* or *y* on the Lord's Day?" Often, the questions are framed in such a manner that any attempt to answer them immediately suggests a form of legalism.

Some Christians assume that any suggestion of Sabbath keeping is essentially legalistic and belongs to the period of the Old Testament. Others will respond by pointing out that Reformed Confessions assume some continuity, arguing that the Ten Commandments (not Nine Commandments) continue to oper-ate under the new covenant.[8] *Some* form of Sabbath keeping must therefore be necessary.

Perhaps a larger perspective is necessary. What obligation do Christians have to law keeping?

Are Christians obligated to keep the moral law? A negative answer here will find us on the wrong side of something that Jesus makes very clear:

If you love me, you will keep my commandments. (John 14:15)

We are obligated to obey everything God commands. And obedience results in joy. That is what Isaiah is insisting in this chapter. There is an essential delight about walking in the paths that God has established. Lawbreaking never ultimately satisfies. Listen to the perspective of the psalmist:

The law of the Lord is perfect,
    reviving the soul;
the testimony of the Lord is sure,

> making wise the simple;
> the precepts of the LORD are right,
>     rejoicing the heart;
> the commandment of the LORD is pure,
>     enlightening the eyes;
> the fear of the LORD is clean,
>     enduring forever;
> the rules of the LORD are true,
>     and righteous altogether.
> More to be desired are they than gold,
>     even much fine gold;
> sweeter also than honey
>     and drippings of the honeycomb.
> Moreover, by them is your servant warned;
>     in keeping them there is great reward. (Ps. 19:7–11)

Note what the psalmist says of God's law (testimony, precepts, commandment): "in keeping them there is great reward." This is true generally of God's law, and it is especially true of the law pertaining to the Sabbath.

## THE SABBATH WAS MADE FOR MAN

The Sabbath is, after all, a creation ordinance. It is part of the created rhythm of the cycle of the first week. Work is followed by a day of rest. In the new covenant, and following perhaps a gospel logic, the order is reversed: rest is followed by work.

To approach this issue of Sabbath keeping from the perspective of "What is God forbidding me to do on the Sabbath?" is essentially wrongheaded. It is a bit like Satan's suggestion in the original temptation in Eden. If God prohibits eating from *one* tree, He might as well prohibit eating from *all* trees. Hence Satan's statement to Eve that *all* trees were out of bounds (Gen. 3:1). The very form of the question suggests that God doesn't really want His creatures to experience any real joy at all. The additional restrictions Satan imposed revealed him to be a legalist at heart.

And legalists never experience joy.

Do we ever think of the Sabbath (Lord's Day) as "a delight"?

And it is not the Sabbath itself that is the ultimate delight but the God whom we meet in worship on the Sabbath. *He* is our chief delight. The Sabbath brings us near to Him and He to us. And there can be no greater joy than that.

It is God's gift to ensure our liberty from the slavery of the unrelenting demands of work. The gift of the Sabbath is the gift of a day given to worship and rest and the blessings that flow from it. It is the greatest gift imaginable. To doubt it suggests we have never really known the blessings of God-centered worship and the freedom and joy that it brings.

The Sabbath is designed as help for the weary. It provides a taste of gospel rest and a foretaste of eternal rest.

> Then shall your light break forth like the dawn,
>> and your healing shall spring up speedily;
> your righteousness shall go before you;
>> the glory of the LORD shall be your rear guard.
> Then you shall call, and the LORD will answer;
>> you shall cry, and he will say, "Here I am."

If you take away the yoke from your midst,
> the pointing of the finger, and speaking wickedness,

if you pour yourself out for the hungry
> and satisfy the desire of the afflicted,

then shall your light rise in the darkness
> and your gloom be as the noonday.

And the LORD will guide you continually
> and satisfy your desire in scorched places
>
> and make your bones strong;

and you shall be like a watered garden,
> like a spring of water,
>
> whose waters do not fail.

And your ancient ruins shall be rebuilt;
> you shall raise up the foundations of many generations;

you shall be called the repairer of the breach,
> the restorer of streets to dwell in. (Isa. 58:8–12)

What can I expect if I give a day a week to worship God? Follow the prophet's line of reasoning for a minute and ask yourself, "Do I know anything of this?"

- Fresh beginnings, like a new dawn.
- Healing and restoration. The word for "healing" is used for new flesh where a wound exists. Do I ever think of the Sabbath as a place where I can be spiritually healed?
- Gospel security that comes from knowing we are considered "righteous." A sense of being in a right relationship with God. Earlier in chapter 53, Isaiah had spoken of the

Servant who will "make many to be accounted righteous" (Isa. 53:11).

- Protection from our enemy in the form of the Lord's "glory"—His personal presence as our rearguard. For in meeting the Lord in worship, it is as though we are given assurance that "He's got our back." Protection indeed!
- Communion with God. You pray and He answers and says, "Here I am." As Alec Motyer puts it, "Answered prayer is not like sending a food parcel; it is like a home visit by the doctor."[9]
- Guidance. "And the LORD will guide you continually" (Isa. 58:11). The reassurance that at every step there is wisdom and instruction as to the way forward.
- Strength: "He will make your bones strong" (Isa. 58:11).
- Refreshment. Like a well-watered garden.
- Rebuilding. This anticipates the rebuilding of Jerusalem following the exile, as well as the New Jerusalem that is yet to come.

All this from a Sabbath? Yes, and more.
Strength for the weary from God's special day.

# 7

# MY DELIGHT

# IS IN HER

You shall be a crown of beauty in the hand of the LORD,
> and a royal diadem in the hand of your God.

You shall no more be termed Forsaken,
> and your land shall no more be termed Desolate,

but you shall be called My Delight Is in Her,
> and your land Married;

for the LORD delights in you,
> and your land shall be married. (Isa. 62:3–4)

We are meant to experience joy. True and lasting joy that comes from knowing God and knowing ourselves. A tangible, irrepressible joy.

Isaiah 61:10–62:7 is the third of the "Songs of the Anointed One"[1] and depicts the joyful scene of a bridegroom and his bride:

I will greatly rejoice in the LORD;
my soul shall exult in my God. (Isa. 61:10)

There are two reasons for this joy. The first is associated with *the bridegroom's clothes.*

Yes, clothes!

When I was a very young minister, I made a comment about a colleague who always appeared smartly dressed, no matter what the occasion. At first, I mistook this for vanity, but then he made the comment, "You are what you wear."

There is some truth in this. There are times when it might be appropriate to be casual. But his point was well taken. Clothes do send a statement—formal, casual, respectful, scruffy, and, perhaps in some instances, an indication of rebellion and moral confusion.

The Anointed One is wearing special clothes: "garments of salvation," "the robe of righteousness," and a priest's headdress (Isa. 61:10). And why the formal regalia? The mention of "bridegroom" and "bride" signal that this is a wedding (Isa. 61:10).

Inappropriate clothing can cause an international crisis. In a recent depiction of Queen Elizabeth II titled *The Crown,* attention was drawn to Colonel Gamal Abdel Nasser Hussein (later president) of Egypt. In 1954, the colonel was invited to a formal dinner with Sir Anthony Eden, the British foreign secretary who was visiting his country's embassy in Cairo. Sir Anthony was undertaking delicate negotiations with Colonel Nasser concerning the Aswan Dam, a project related to the perpetual political morass of the bigger Suez Canal issue. When Nasser showed up at the British embassy in full military uniform, an international crisis almost ensued. He was unaware that the dinner was to be a formal event and was embarrassed to be greeted by Sir Anthony, who was wearing black tie. The colonel took the misunderstanding to be a deliberate attempt to humiliate him.

## WEDDING CLOTHES

The Anointed One in Isaiah's poem is drawing attention to His wedding clothes. We tend to think of the pain and suffering associated with Jesus' death—the bloody carnage that accompanied the public flogging and the crucifixion that followed.

Here, in this section of Isaiah's prophecy, Jesus is thinking of His wedding clothes. The Suffering Servant is also the bridegroom at His wedding with His people, His bride, His church. The focus is not so much the blood-stained seamless robe He wore on His way to Calvary, but on His wedding attire. This is how much we mean to Him! We see the blood; He sees His beautiful bride.

Two specific images emerge that describe His attire:

- "The garments of salvation." When Jesus appeared to Joshua, He did so as "commander of the army of the LORD" (Josh. 5:14). He was dressed in battle gear. His garments suggest He has power and might to accomplish His task.
- "A robe of righteousness." He alone can wear this robe, for He alone is truly righteous. He came to "fulfill all righteousness" (Matt. 3:15). By faith this righteousness is reckoned ours: "For our sake he made him to be sin who

knew no sin, so that in him we might become the righteousness of God" (2 Cor. 5:21). The Suffering Servant and "righteous one" will "make many to be accounted righteous, and he shall bear their iniquities" (Isa. 53:11). Dressed in this robe, we may stand firm and secure amidst the threats and accusations of Satan and the world. We are reckoned righteous in Christ—as righteous as Christ Himself.

Jesus, Thy blood and righteousness
My beauty are, my glorious dress;
'Midst flaming worlds, in these arrayed,
With joy shall I lift up my head.

Bold shall I stand in Thy great day;
For who aught to my charge shall lay?
Fully absolved through these I am
From sin and fear, from guilt and shame.[2]

## SUCCESS

If the first reason for joy is associated with the Anointed One's clothes, the second is associated with the success of His mission.

For as the earth brings forth its sprouts,
and as a garden causes what is sown in it to sprout up,
so the Lord GOD will cause righteousness and praise
to sprout up before all the nations. (Isa. 61:11)

As sure as seeds sprout and grow and produce plants and vegetation, so too the work of the Anointed is bound to succeed. The imputed righteousness of the "righteous one" will in turn produce righteousness in His bride, considered here again to have an international identity—"all nations."

And there is joy for the bride, too.

> You shall no more be termed Forsaken,
>> and your land shall no more be termed Desolate,
> but you shall be called My Delight Is in Her,
>> and your land Married;
> for the LORD delights in you,
>> and your land shall be married.
> For as a young man marries a young woman,
>> so shall your sons marry you,
> and as the bridegroom rejoices over the bride,
>> so shall your God rejoice over you. (Isa. 62:4–5)

As is traditional in marriage, the bride receives a new name. No longer is she called "Forsaken" and "Desolate" but "My Delight Is in Her" (*Hephzibah*) and "Married" (*Beulah*). These two words correspond to the wedding and the honeymoon. And continuing the theme of marriage, Alec Motyer comments, "Zion's sons make their marriage vow to their bride 'to love and to cherish,' to give themselves in devoted service to the welfare of Zion, and the Lord goes on honeymoon with his people, rejoicing over them."[3]

The theme is continued in the New Testament in the form of the marriage supper of the Lamb depicted in Revelation 19:

Then I heard what seemed to be the voice of a great multitude, like the roar of many waters and like the sound of mighty peals of thunder, crying out,

"Hallelujah!
For the Lord our God
    the Almighty reigns.
Let us rejoice and exult
    and give him the glory,
for the marriage of the Lamb has come,
    and his Bride has made herself ready;
it was granted her to clothe herself
    with fine linen, bright and pure." (Rev. 19:6–8)

This is also a theme taken up elsewhere in the New Testament.

Husbands, love your wives, as Christ loved the church and gave himself up for her, that he might sanctify her, having cleansed her by the washing of water with the word, so that he might present the church to himself in splendor, without spot or wrinkle or any such thing, that she might be holy and without blemish. (Eph. 5:25–27)

And I saw the holy city, new Jerusalem, coming down out of heaven from God, prepared as a bride adorned for her husband. . . . Then came one of the seven angels who had the seven bowls full of the seven last plagues and spoke to me, saying, "Come, I will show you the Bride, the wife of the Lamb." (Rev. 21:2, 9)

We are the Anointed One's bride.

Joy springs from the knowledge and assurance that we are loved and cherished.

Loved by God.

Eternally loved with a love that is unimaginably costly.

A love that can never diminish.

## COMMITMENT

If joy is one theme of this song, commitment is another. And like the first theme, this one also has two parts.

In the first part, the Anointed One is depicted as saying (twice), "I will not keep silent":

> For Zion's sake I will not keep silent,
>     and for Jerusalem's sake I will not be quiet,
> until her righteousness goes forth as brightness,
>     and her salvation as a burning torch.
> The nations shall see your righteousness,
>     and all the kings your glory,
> and you shall be called by a new name
>     that the mouth of the LORD will give.
> You shall be a crown of beauty in the hand of the LORD,
>     and a royal diadem in the hand of your God. (Isa. 62:1–3)

## THE PRAYING MEDIATOR

"I will not keep silent." The Anointed One is ceaseless in His prayers on behalf of His bride. He "always lives to make intercession for them" (Heb. 7:25).[4] "We have an advocate with the Father, Jesus Christ the righteous" (1 John 2:1). Night and day, He intercedes on behalf of His own. He will not stop until His people display the righteousness that He has won on their behalf and now wishes to impute to them.

How should we think of the intercession of Christ?

To begin with, we should avoid thinking that the Father is reluctant to bestow His blessing on us. A caricature exists that the Son must in some way cajole His Father in order to provide us with the blessings He has won for us. Such a thought suggests that the Father is essentially indifferent, even hostile to us, but that in response to His Son's pleas, He yields.

Nothing could be further from the truth. It is because of the Father's love for us that the Son came in the first place.

> For God so loved the world, that he gave his only Son, that whoever believes in him should not perish but have eternal life. (John 3:16)

Nothing distorts our understanding of the Trinity more than the notion that the affection of one person of the Godhead is essentially different from the affection of another. The essential unity of God demands that all three persons of the Godhead essentially desire the same thing.

One of the most important contributions of the early church fathers was the insistence that the external operations of God cannot be divided. Using a Latin formula, they insisted on the following: *Opera trinitatis ad extra indivisa sunt* (the external actions of the Trinity cannot be divided).

Though it is cumbersome to us, and made more so by the use of Latin, the essence of this formula speaks of something sublime indeed. The Father, the Son, and the Holy Spirit equally desire our salvation and ultimate joy. To say otherwise would irreparably divide the Holy Trinity.

Another thought emerges as we contemplate the intercession of Jesus on behalf of His own people.

As Mediator and last Adam, Jesus provides the righteousness necessary for us to be reconciled to God. As Mediator, He continues to ensure that all He has accomplished *for us* is also meticulously applied *to us*.

Intercession was a vital part of the Mediator's life on earth. Think of John 17, the High Priestly Prayer. There, in the upper room, and in the hearing of His disciples, Jesus prayed on behalf of His people. But that intercession did not cease by virtue of Christ's exaltation. Jesus is still the Mediator. And He continues to intercede on our behalf.

## THE CROWN

One further thought: believers are considered "a crown":

> You shall be a crown of beauty in the hand of the LORD,
>     and a royal diadem in the hand of your God. (Isa. 62:3)

A beautiful crown. For all the world to see. The Lord regards His people as "the sign to the watching world that he is king."[5]

A sign. Is that how we think of ourselves? And lest we fall into the trap of thinking we are hardly good enough to be signs to the world, we should remind ourselves immediately that we are not, and never will be, good enough. We are a crown because, in union with Christ, we are reckoned to be kings. We have royal blood. We are the King's children, His royal progeny. And therefore heirs along with Christ:

> For you did not receive the spirit of slavery to fall back into fear, but you have received the Spirit of adoption as sons, by whom we cry, "Abba! Father!" The Spirit himself bears witness with our spirit that we are children of God, and if children, then heirs—heirs of God and fellow heirs with Christ, provided we suffer with him in order that we may also be glorified with him. (Rom. 8:15–17)

## WATCHMEN

Jesus prays. And we must pray too. This is the theme of the closing verses of the Song in Isaiah 62.

> On your walls, O Jerusalem,
>     I have set watchmen;
> all the day and all the night
>     they shall never be silent.
> You who put the LORD in remembrance,
>     take no rest,
> and give him no rest
>     until he establishes Jerusalem
>     and makes it a praise in the earth. (Isa. 62:6–7)

This is a call to unceasing prayer ("day" and "night"). Paul urges the Thessalonians to "pray without ceasing" (1 Thess. 5:17).

Until His kingdom comes.

Strength is found in prayer.

# 8

# NEW HEAVENS AND NEW EARTH

For behold, I create new heavens
    and a new earth,
and the former things shall not be remembered
    or come into mind. (Isa. 65:17)

For as the new heavens and the new earth
    that I make
shall remain before me, says the LORD,
    so shall your offspring and your name remain.
From new moon to new moon,
    and from Sabbath to Sabbath,
all flesh shall come to worship before me,
declares the LORD. (Isa. 66:22–23)

Human beings are hope-shaped. We were created to experience fulfillment. As image bearers of God, we are designed to be explorers, never content with staying still but always reaching forward, inquiring, searching, hoping, grasping.

There is a void, a potential within us that only God can fill. Without this "filling" there is what the author of Ecclesiastes frequently describes as a *hevel*—a pointlessness, a vanity.[1]

Philosophers such as Albert Camus and Jean-Paul Sartre examined the consequence of nineteenth-century liberalism and humanism and concluded that if, indeed, there is no God and we are but accidents "within a universe that is constantly churning," then life has no meaning either. If there is no purpose and no goal, then we have no value. We have emerged from *das Nichtigkeit*—the nothingness—and there is nothing in the future to anticipate.

We are creatures for hope. As fallen creatures, the hope we need is all the more needful. And hope is how Isaiah closes his lengthy prophecy: God intends to create something new:

> For behold, I create new heavens
> and a new earth. (Isa. 65:17)

The future could not be grander than the description Isaiah gives of God's intended purpose for this world. A new world order!

But what exactly is the promise here? What kind of new order? And for whom?

Isaiah makes it clear: this new world order is not for everyone. In keeping with what the Bible declares elsewhere, the prophet speaks of two groups of people and two distinct destinies—one destiny is for those who are "sought" by the Lord (and referred to as "my servants," "my people," and "my chosen"; Isa. 65:8, 9, 10, 13, 14) and the other for those "who do not seek" Him (Isa. 65:1). The first group is promised food and drink, joy and gladness. The second group is threatened with hunger and thirst, pain, and "breaking of spirit" (Isa. 65:13–14).

God's people, like Abram (Abraham), are going to be given a new name: "his servants he will call by another name" (Isa. 65:15). We are not told what this name is, but, like the earlier references to *Hephzibah* (My Delight Is in Her) and *Beulah* (Married) (Isa. 62:4), it seems to promise a new nature and new horizons of expectation.

But how and when will such promises come about? Isaiah 65:17–25 provides the answer:

"For behold, I create new heavens
    and a new earth,
and the former things shall not be remembered
    or come into mind.
But be glad and rejoice forever
    in that which I create;
for behold, I create Jerusalem to be a joy,
    and her people to be a gladness.
I will rejoice in Jerusalem
    and be glad in my people;
no more shall be heard in it the sound of weeping
    and the cry of distress.
No more shall there be in it
    an infant who lives but a few days,
    or an old man who does not fill out his days,
for the young man shall die a hundred years old,
    and the sinner a hundred years old shall be accursed.
They shall build houses and inhabit them;
    they shall plant vineyards and eat their fruit.

They shall not build and another inhabit;
    they shall not plant and another eat;
for like the days of a tree shall the days of my people be,
    and my chosen shall long enjoy the work of their hands.
They shall not labor in vain
    or bear children for calamity,
for they shall be the offspring of the blessed of the LORD,
    and their descendants with them.
Before they call I will answer;
    while they are yet speaking I will hear.
The wolf and the lamb shall graze together;
    the lion shall eat straw like the ox,
    and dust shall be the serpent's food.
They shall not hurt or destroy
    in all my holy mountain,"
says the LORD.

## A NEW CREATION

Three times the Lord in Isaiah employs the verb "create"—the same Hebrew verb Moses employs in the opening verse of Genesis:

For behold, I create new heavens and a new earth. . . . I create. . . . For behold, I create. . . . (Isa. 65:17–18)

In the beginning, God created the heavens and the earth. (Gen. 1:1)

The Bible begins with theism. The reason for the universe—plants, dogs, stars, humans, everything—is God. The universe and all that is in it did not emerge spontaneously out of nothing by itself. Spontaneous generation—the idea that the universe exploded into being by itself—effectively maintains that *nothing* produces *something*. This is philosophical nonsense. It is, in fact, a very difficult notion to grasp (let alone believe) that nothing has the inherent power to produce everything. Of course, we could postulate that there was *something* in being before the universe. A gas. Gravity. Electromagnetism. And this "something" produces everything. It is a testimony to the folly of humankind that such a notion is given serious academic consideration. But it is nonsense—non-*sense*.

Either there was nothing, or there was something, or there was God. The Bible is clear. Before the universe existed, there was (is) God. The universe comes into being as a result of His will, His power, His creative act. He spoke it into being, bringing the cosmos *ex nihilo*—out of nothing.

And at the end of the age, at some point in the future, God will do a similar creating act. He will speak a new heavens and a new earth into existence.

> For behold, I create new heavens
> and a new earth,
> and the former things shall not be remembered
> or come into mind.
> But be glad and rejoice forever
> in that which I create. (Isa. 65:17–18)

Question:    What happens when a believer dies?
Answer:    The souls of believers are at their death made perfect in holiness, and do immediately pass into glory; and their

bodies, being still united to Christ, do rest in their graves till the resurrection.[2]

Put in simpler (though less accurate) terms, the souls of believers go to heaven when they die. Using the term "heaven" in this way signals what we often mean when we speak of heaven. Technically, this is the "intermediate state"—what Jesus meant when He replied to the dying thief at His side on the cross, "Truly, I say to you, today you will be with me in paradise" (Luke 23:43).

This is a priceless truth and one that needs to be affirmed in the face of the skepticism of the modern age. But it is not the truth that is being affirmed in this passage. It is not "heaven" but "heavens" that is in view in Isaiah 65. It is the same reference as in Genesis 1. The planetary system, the stars. All that can be seen in the night sky and more. God is going to create a "new heavens."

Not only that, He will also create a new earth that is as physical, temporal, and spatial as the present one.

I have lost count of the number of times I have been asked, "Are there dogs in heaven?" I am asked the question, partly, because of my love for these four-legged creatures. I cannot imagine life without them. And those who ask me this question often want an answer to a more precise question: "Will *my* dog be in heaven?"

I am certain that there will be dogs "in heaven"—if by "heaven" we actually mean "the new heavens and new earth" of which Isaiah speaks in chapter 65 of his prophecy. I am not sure of the answer to the question, "Will *my* dog be in heaven?" except I am certain that our joy will be complete in the new heavens and new earth. I am certain that there will be dogs there. And cats (yes!). And fish. And birds. And every creature that God has ever created. And perhaps some that are new to us.

Too often we think of our future existence as somewhat ethereal, ghostly . . . floating on clouds, perhaps. And this is not what the Bible predicts at all. The future existence will be as physical and tangible as this one, full of inquiry, discovery, and exploration.

This new existence will be perfect. The "former things shall not be remembered" (Isa. 65:17)—the "former things" mentioned in the previous verse and referred to as "the former troubles" (Isa. 65:16). There will be no lasting memory of the troubles that encompass our current lives in this world.

Does this mean that we will have no memory of anything bad? I don't think this is what it means. Surely, we will have a recollection of the cross—the brutality and inhumanity done to our Lord during His life and in His death upon the cross. There will be no forgetting that.

Perhaps what is intended here is that the good—the joy and fullness of life in the new heavens and new earth—will so outweigh the evil of our current existence that the latter will have no opportunity to rise and haunt us.

The new heavens and earth will also be eternal. God will create it to last forever.

What does *forever* mean? In the movie *Alice in Wonderland*, Alice asks the White Rabbit, "How long is forever?" "Sometimes, just one second," he answers.[3] Promises of fidelity made here and now are sometimes broken within a second. But God's promises can never be broken. Forever means—*forever*!

## A NEW CITY

It is perhaps difficult for us to fully imagine what Jerusalem meant to Old Testament believers. It was more than just a city, or even a capital city. Jerusalem was the one place on earth where sin could be atoned for and true worship offered. The emotional and spiritual significance of Jerusalem was incalculable. Believers living far away were prepared to sacrifice time and energy to make annual pilgrimages to this city.

When God says, "I create Jerusalem. . . . I will rejoice in Jerusalem" (Isa. 65:18–19), He does so in a context where the readers of the prophecy would soon experience enforced exile from the city. Babylonian soldiers would ransack and pillage the city, tearing down its walls and destroying its temple. And those in exile would be unable to sing a song of worship when taunted to do so:

> By the waters of Babylon,
> > there we sat down and wept,
> > when we remembered Zion.
> On the willows there
> > we hung up our lyres.
> For there our captors
> > required of us songs,
> and our tormentors, mirth, saying,
> > "Sing us one of the songs of Zion!"
> How shall we sing the Lord's song
> > in a foreign land?
> If I forget you, O Jerusalem,

let my right hand forget its skill!
Let my tongue stick to the roof of my mouth,
    if I do not remember you,
if I do not set Jerusalem
    above my highest joy! (Ps. 137:1–6)

The city of Babel became a symbol of defiance with its towering ziggurat (Gen. 11). And Isaiah had promised earlier a new city
in place of Babylon (Isa. 26).

Cities are places of great potential and influence. They bring
together talent and enterprise that enable the collective to outdo
what the rural individual might achieve. Urban development
projects and inner-city revitalization are concepts with which we
are familiar as attempts to bring life and culture back into the city.
There are examples where such social reconstruction has proved
successful up to a point.

But God's vision is far greater than a typical urban renewal
project. The city God intends to create will not have the sound
of crying due to illness and death. In an extended metaphor, the
prophet thinks of infant mortality and the death of young men.

No more shall be heard in it the sound of weeping
    and the cry of distress.
No more shall there be in it
    an infant who lives but a few days,
    or an old man who does not fill out his days,
for the young man shall die a hundred years old,
    and the sinner a hundred years old shall be accursed.
    (Isa. 65:19–20)

Isaiah is using a metaphor for longevity of life. Who, after all, can grasp "forever"? The prophet does not intend to suggest that people will die in the new heavens and earth. The idea is one of fulfillment. We sometimes speak of those who die "before their time"—before they have had an opportunity to achieve their potential and make a mark for themselves. In the new heavens and earth, everyone—"my people" (Isa. 65:19)—will live out the fullness that God always intended them to achieve.

## A NEW COMMUNITY

A new creation. A new city. And a new community.

> "They shall build houses and inhabit them;
>    they shall plant vineyards and eat their fruit.
> They shall not build and another inhabit;
>    they shall not plant and another eat;
> for like the days of a tree shall the days of my people be,
>    and my chosen shall long enjoy the work of their hands.
> They shall not labor in vain
>    or bear children for calamity,
> for they shall be the offspring of the blessed of the LORD,
>    and their descendants with them.
> Before they call I will answer;
>    while they are yet speaking I will hear.
> The wolf and the lamb shall graze together;
>    the lion shall eat straw like the ox,
>    and dust shall be the serpent's food.

They shall not hurt or destroy
    in all my holy mountain,"
says the LORD. (Isa. 65:21–25)

Employing a series of pictures to express the nature of this new community, Isaiah suggests the following:

- A life of *fruitfulness* and *fulfillment*. Instead of the frustration that mars our present existence, in the new heavens and new earth we will reap the fruits of our labors—occupying the buildings we erect and eating the crops we sow and cultivate (Isa. 65:21–22). It is as if the prophet is describing an existence in which, as Motyer suggests, life is enjoyed to the maximum.[4]

Imagine what it would be like to live without frustration, disappointment, or injustice. Truth is, we find it almost impossible to imagine such an existence. Our current experience is so marred by the pointlessness and vanity described so eloquently in Ecclesiastes with its repeated outbursts—"all is vanity!"—that we might be tempted to doubt such an existence is possible. But this would be to yield to unbelief rather than faith.

- A life *free from the trauma of pain and suffering*. The picture the Bible employs is the pain of watching our children suffer. And can there be any greater pain than this? As parents or grandparents, we would do almost anything to relieve the suffering our children or grandchildren experience.

When Donald Grey Barnhouse, the former minister of Tenth Presbyterian Church, lost his wife, he found himself struggling to ease the pain his young daughter felt by the loss of her mother. They were driving one day, and a large moving truck passed them. The dark shadow of the truck passed over them. Here is what Barnhouse said:

> "Would you rather be run over by a truck, or by its shadow?" His daughter replied, "By the shadow of course. That can't hurt us at all." Dr. Barnhouse replied, "Right. If the truck doesn't hit you, but only its shadow, then you are fine. Well, it was only the shadow of death that went over your mother. She's actually alive—more alive than we are. And that's because two thousand years ago, the real truck of death hit Jesus. And because death crushed Jesus, and we believe in him, now the only thing that can come over us is the shadow of death, and the shadow of death is but my entrance into glory."[5]

God intends for us an existence in which we will never die or experience the pain of loss or suffering. We may not believe that such a thing is possible. But that, too, is to yield to unbelief rather than to faith.

- A life where *all creation exists in perfect harmony and communion.* Two pictures emerge:

The first is a picture of intimate communion with God. Using the idea of prayer, Isaiah imagines what it will be like to always ask for that which perfectly conforms to the Lord's will. So much of praying here and now is muddled because we are not clear as to God's will in the matter. "If it be Your will," we say. But in this new existence, our asking and God's granting will be simultaneous: "While they are yet speaking I will hear" (Isa. 65:24). It is a picture, of course. But it suggests the most intense intimacy. We will have such an understanding of what is right that we will not ask for that which does not conform to His will. We may not believe such a thing is possible. But that, too, is to yield to unbelief rather than to faith.

The second picture takes us back to an earlier chapter in Isaiah, where carnivorous animals are lying down together without threat of any kind:

> The wolf shall dwell with the lamb,
>     and the leopard shall lie down with the young goat,
> and the calf and the lion and the fattened calf together;
>     and a little child shall lead them.
> The cow and the bear shall graze;
>     their young shall lie down together;
>     and the lion shall eat straw like the ox.
> The nursing child shall play over the hole of the cobra,
>     and the weaned child shall put his hand on the adder's den.
> They shall not hurt or destroy
>     in all my holy mountain;
> for the earth shall be full of the knowledge of the LORD
>     as the waters cover the sea. (Isa. 11:6–9)

Wolves and lambs, leopards and goats grazing together. The curse of Genesis 3:14–15 has been lifted. Carnivores have become herbivores. And little children seem safe in their presence.

The Apostle Peter reflected on these closing accounts of a "new heavens and new earth" in his second epistle. And what is Peter's point in citing this passage? That we should be holy.

> Since all these things are thus to be dissolved, what sort of people ought you to be in lives of holiness and godliness, waiting for and hastening the coming of the day of God, because of which the heavens will be set on fire and dissolved, and the heavenly bodies will melt as they burn! But according to his promise we are waiting for new heavens and a new earth in which righteousness dwells. (2 Peter 3:11–13)

Knowing that such a glorious future awaits us as God's children, we should live in a manner that anticipates it. That's Peter's point.

Live for that which lasts. Don't be satisfied with things that ultimately have no lasting value.

Very few people live entirely for the present. Most have aspirations and desires that reflect a need for something beyond today, or even tomorrow. We strive to overcome our finiteness in order to create something that lasts.

Some immerse themselves in creating wealth that far outweighs their current or future need. Others strive to build a reputation for themselves, a legacy that ensures they will be remembered long after they have left this world. Still others build massive collections (rare books, memorabilia from the '60s, antique cars) and swagger in the superiority that such a collection brings. In Peter's time, false teachers did different things. They lined their pockets with cash, boasted in their prowess at interpreting Paul's more difficult statements, elevated themselves above criticism, and gave themselves to sexual license (see 2 Peter 2:10, 14–16, 18; 3:16). To which Peter said, "It's all going to be burned up."

Giving yourself to things that ultimately have no lasting value will ultimately destroy you.

Instead, and by the grace of God, give yourself to what *really* lasts: the new heavens and new earth.

This alone provides strength for the weary.

# NOTES

## Preface

1. Hebrew *hinnam*.

2. It was what the disciples thought when Jesus lay sleeping in the storm-tossed boat on the Sea of Galilee: "Do you not care that we are perishing?" (Mark 4:38).

3. Alec Motyer, *Isaiah*, Tyndale Old Testament Commentaries (hereafter TOTC) (Leicester, England: InterVarsity Press, 1999); *The Prophecy of Isaiah* (hereafter TPI) (Leicester, England: InterVarsity Press, 1993); *Isaiah by the Day: A New Devotional Translation* (Fearn, Ross-shire, Scotland: Christian Focus, 2011).

## 1. Strength for the Weary

1. This is not the place for an in-depth analysis of the structure of Isaiah's prophecy. Suffice it to say that I regard the book as one unified composition. By "second half" I simply mean chapters 40–66. The structure of Isaiah is far more complex, of course, and those who require a more scholarly analysis should read Alec Motyer's analysis in the introduction to TOTC, 15–18.

2. Westminster Confession of Faith 18.4.

3. Motyer, TOTC, 241.

4. Motyer, TOTC, 242.

5. *Luther: Letters of Spiritual Counsel*, trans. and ed. Theodore G. Tappert (Vancouver, British Columbia: Regent College Publishing, 1960), 146–47.

6. J.B. Phillips, *Your God is Too Small* (New York: Touchstone, 2004).

7. J.I. Packer and O.R. Johnston, eds., *Martin Luther, The Bondage of the Will 1525* (Westwood, N.J.: Fleming Revell, 1957), 87. These words are sometimes misunderstood, as though Luther was correcting a view that made too little of

God's transcendence. Luther, however, was doing the very opposite. Erasmus had raised the scholastic notion of whether God could be present in the hole of a dung beetle and concluded that this was beneath him. On the contrary, Luther remarked, God is everywhere. He condescended to enter the womb of a young girl called Mary. He became flesh and dwelt among us (John 1:14).

8. This verse ("Even youths shall faint and be weary") uses a different Hebrew word from Isaiah 40:28 ("He does not . . . grow weary") that suggests exhaustion.

9. The word "emptiness" (Hebrew *tohu*) is rendered "void" in Gen. 1:2 ("The earth was without form and void," without meaning or purpose).

10. Cf. Job 40:4: "Behold, I am of small account; what shall I answer you? I lay my hand on my mouth."

11. Motyer, TOTC, 246.

12. C.S. Lewis, *The Last Battle* (New York: MacMillan, 1970), 147–48.

## 2. Who Rules the World?

1. The word "blind" is in the plural and refers to the "nations" of Isaiah 42:6–7.

2. The word "blind" in this verse is in the singular and refers to Israel.

3. *The Complete Works of Stephen Charnock*, 5 vols., (Edinburgh, Scotland: Banner of Truth, 2010), 4:81. The quotation occurs in a sermon on John 17:3.

4. Also in Isaiah 43:7.

5. "We are the clay, and you are our potter" (Isa. 64:8).

6. Isaiah 43:7; cf. Genesis 1:31.

7. Motyer, TPI, 333.

8. In Israel's case, the price was "Egypt": "I give Egypt as your ransom, Cush and Seba in exchange for you" (Isa. 43:3). Cush and Seba lay in Egypt's southernmost territory.

9. "Redeemed, How I Love to Proclaim It!," Fanny Crosby, 1872.

10. John Calvin, *Institutes of the Christian Religion*, trans. Ford Lewis Battles, 2 vols., Library of Christian Classics 20–21 (Philadelphia: Westminster John Knox, 1960), 108 [1.11.8].

11. Attributed to Robert Keen, c. 1787.

## 3. I Am the Only God There Is

1. *Twice* in Isaiah 44:28–45:1.

2. The "Cyrus prophecy" covers the section Isaiah 44:24–45:7.

3. See, for example, *Evidence for the Bible*, eds. Clive Anderson and Brian Edwards (Leominster, England: Day One, 2014), 97.

4. "For truly, I say to you, until heaven and earth pass away, not an iota, not a dot, will pass from the Law until all is accomplished" (Matt. 5:18).

5. C.S. Lewis, *Miracles* (New York: Simon & Schuster, 1996), 169.

6. Kevin DeYoung, *Taking God at His Word: Why the Bible Is Knowable, Necessary, and Enough, and What That Means for You and Me* (Wheaton, Ill.: Crossway, 2016), 122.

7. Cited by W.P. Stephens, *Zwingli: An Introduction to His Thought* (Oxford, England: Oxford University Press, 1992), 48.

8. I am employing the more current terms here for what in the past were termed God's "decretive" will and His "preceptive" will.

9. David Wells, *God in the Wasteland* (Grand Rapids, Mich.: Eerdmans, 1994), 52.

10. Neil Postman, *Amusing Ourselves to Death: Public Discourse in the Age of Show Business* (New York: Penguin, 1985), vii–viii. Cited in D.A. Carson, *The Gagging of God: Christianity Confronts Pluralism* (Leicester, England: Apollos, 1996), 463–64.

## 4. The Burden-Bearing God

1. After the Civil War, Lee served as president of the college from 1865 to 1870, and afterward the college was renamed Washington and Lee. Today it is called Washington and Lee University.

2. Jaques Ellul, *Subversion and Christianity* (Grand Rapids, Mich.: Eedrmans, 1986). Cited by Terry Lindvall, *God Mocks: A History of Religious Satire from the Hebrew Prophets to Stephen Colbert* (New York: New York University Press, 2015), 3.

3. Timothy Keller, *Counterfeit Gods: The Empty Promises of Money, Sex and Power, and the Only Hope That Matters* (New York: Dutton, 2009), 75.

4. The refrain of the hymn "In Loving-kindness Jesus Came" by Charles H. Gabriel (1910).

5. A statement J.I. Packer made in his book, *Finishing Our Course with Joy: Guidance from God for Engaging with Our Aging* (Wheaton, Ill.: Crossway, 2014), 88.

## Interlude: The Servant, Jesus

1. The Reformers were fond of saying that salvation is *extra nos*, "from outside ourselves."

2. *Hesed* in the Hebrew is a word that epitomizes Yahweh's special love for His people.

3. See Isaiah 2:2–4 and 11:6–9.

4. See Isaiah 9:1–7, especially verse 7: "Of the increase of his government and of peace there will be no end, on the throne of David and over his kingdom, to establish it and to uphold it with justice and with righteousness from this time forth and forevermore."

5. On Israel as the servant, see Isaiah 41:8; 49:3.

6. Alec Motyer suggests that the word "justice" in Isaiah 42:1 ("he will bring forth justice to the nations") is best understood as one who brings divine truth to the gentiles. See Motyer, TOTC, 259–60.

## 5. The Waters of Life

1. C.G. Jung, *The Red Book* (New York: Philemon Foundation & W.W. Norton, 2009). Cited in "Shame and the Midbrain Urge to Withdraw" by Frank M. Corrigan, in Ulrich F. Lanius, *Neurobiology and Treatment of Traumatic Dissociation: Towards an Embodied Self* (New York: Springer, 2014), 173.

2. Each of the Servant Songs is followed by a commentary. And befitting the majestic style of the fourth Servant Song (52:13–53:12), this commentary takes up two whole chapters.

3. This is Alec Motyer's translation in *Isaiah by the Day*, 267.

4. The word "peoples" occurs twice, effectively beginning and ending the sentence in the Hebrew (Isa. 55:4).

5. The word "nation" occurs twice in Isaiah 55:5.

6. Two singular forms of the word *hesed* also appear in Psalm 89:24, 28.

7. Mark Noll, *The New Shape of World Christianity: How American Experience Reflects Global Faith* (Downers Grove, Ill.: InterVarsity Academic, 2009), 10.

8. Sinclair B. Ferguson, *A Heart for God* (Edinburgh, Scotland: Banner of Truth, 1987), 36–37.

9. Referring to the effects of Adam's sin on creation, Paul writes, "For the creation was subjected to futility" (Rom. 8:20).

10. Andrew Delbanco, *The Real American Dream: A Meditation on Hope* (Cambridge, Mass.: Harvard University Press, 1999), 1–2.

11. These words form the basis of the opening sentences of Thomas Watson's treatise titled "The Doctrine of Repentance," written in 1668, http://gracegems.org/Watson/repentance1.htm, accessed November 5, 2016.

12. "I Heard the Voice of Jesus Say," Horatius Bonar (1846).

## 6. A Well-Watered Garden

1. "For we hold that one is justified by faith apart from works of the law" (Rom. 3:28).

2. Westminster Confession of Faith 11:2.

3. Martin Luther, *Commentary on Romans*, trans. J. Theodore Mueller (Grand Rapids, Mich.: Zondervan, 1954), xvii.

4. Cited in Romans 3:15–17.

5. See https://www.thegospelcoalition.org/article/election-is-over-lets-get-political, accessed November 10, 2016.

6. Compare Isaiah 58:2–5 and 58:13–14. See Motyer TOTC, 363.

7. We could also translate the opening phrase of verse 13 this way: "If you keep your feet from breaking the Sabbath. . . ."

8. See the appendix in Sinclair Ferguson, *Devoted to God: Blueprints for Sanctification* (Edinburgh, Scotland: Banner of Truth, 1996), 261–70.

9. Motyer, TOTC, 362.

## 7. My Delight Is in Her

1. Four "Servant Songs" (42:1–9; 49:1–13; 50:4–11; 52:13–53:12) are followed by four "Songs of the Anointed One" (59:21; 61:1–4; 61:10–62:7; 63:1–6). The latter songs pick up themes addressed in the Servant Songs.

2. "Jesus, Thy Blood and Righteousness," Count Nicolaus von Zinzendorf (1739).

3. Motyer, TOTC, 381. See Isaiah 62:4–5.

4. Cf. Romans 8:34, "who indeed is interceding for us."

5. Motyer, TOTC, 381.

## 8. New Heavens and New Earth

1. "Vanity of vanities, says the Preacher, vanity of vanities! All is vanity" (Eccl. 1:2).

2. This is the answer to question 37 of the Westminster Shorter Catechism: "What benefits do believers receive from Christ at death?"

3. *Alice in Wonderland*, directed by Tim Burton (Los Angeles: Walt Disney Studios, 2010), DVD. The movie is based on Lewis Carroll's *Alice's Adventure in Wonderland* and *Through the Looking Glass*. The quotation is frequently (and incorrectly) attributed to Lewis Carroll himself.

4. Motyer, TOTC, 399.

5. Cited by Timothy Keller, *Walking with God through Pain and Suffering* (New York: Dutton, 2013), 317.

# SCRIPTURE INDEX

# ABOUT THE AUTHOR

Dr. Derek W.H. Thomas is senior minister of the historic First Presbyterian Church in Columbia, S.C., Chancellor's Professor of Systematic and Pastoral Theology at Reformed Theological Seminary, and a Ligonier Ministries teaching fellow. He previously served as minister of teaching at First Presbyterian Church in Jackson, Miss., and chairman of the theology department at Reformed Theological Seminary in Jackson. A native of Wales, Dr. Thomas is a graduate of the University of Wales (B.Sc.), Reformed Theological Seminary (M.Div), and University of Wales/Lampeter (Ph.D.).

He is author or coauthor of more than twenty books, including *Ichthus: Jesus Christ, God's Son, the Savior* (with Sinclair B. Ferguson), *How the Gospel Brings Us All the Way Home*, *Let's Study Revelation* and *Let's Study Galatians* from the Let's Study series, *Calvin's Teaching on Job*, and *Praying the Savior's Way*.

Dr. Thomas is married to Rosemary. They have two grown children, one granddaughter, and one grandson.